THE CAMPAIGN IN THRACE
1912

THE CAMPAIGN IN THRACE
1912

SIX LECTURES
By
MAJOR P. HOWELL

The Naval & Military Press Ltd

Published by

The Naval & Military Press Ltd
Unit 5 Riverside, Brambleside
Bellbrook Industrial Estate
Uckfield, East Sussex
TN22 1QQ England

Tel: +44 (0)1825 749494

www.naval-military-press.com
www.nmarchive.com

In reprinting in facsimile from the original, any imperfections are inevitably reproduced and the quality may fall short of modern type and cartographic standards.

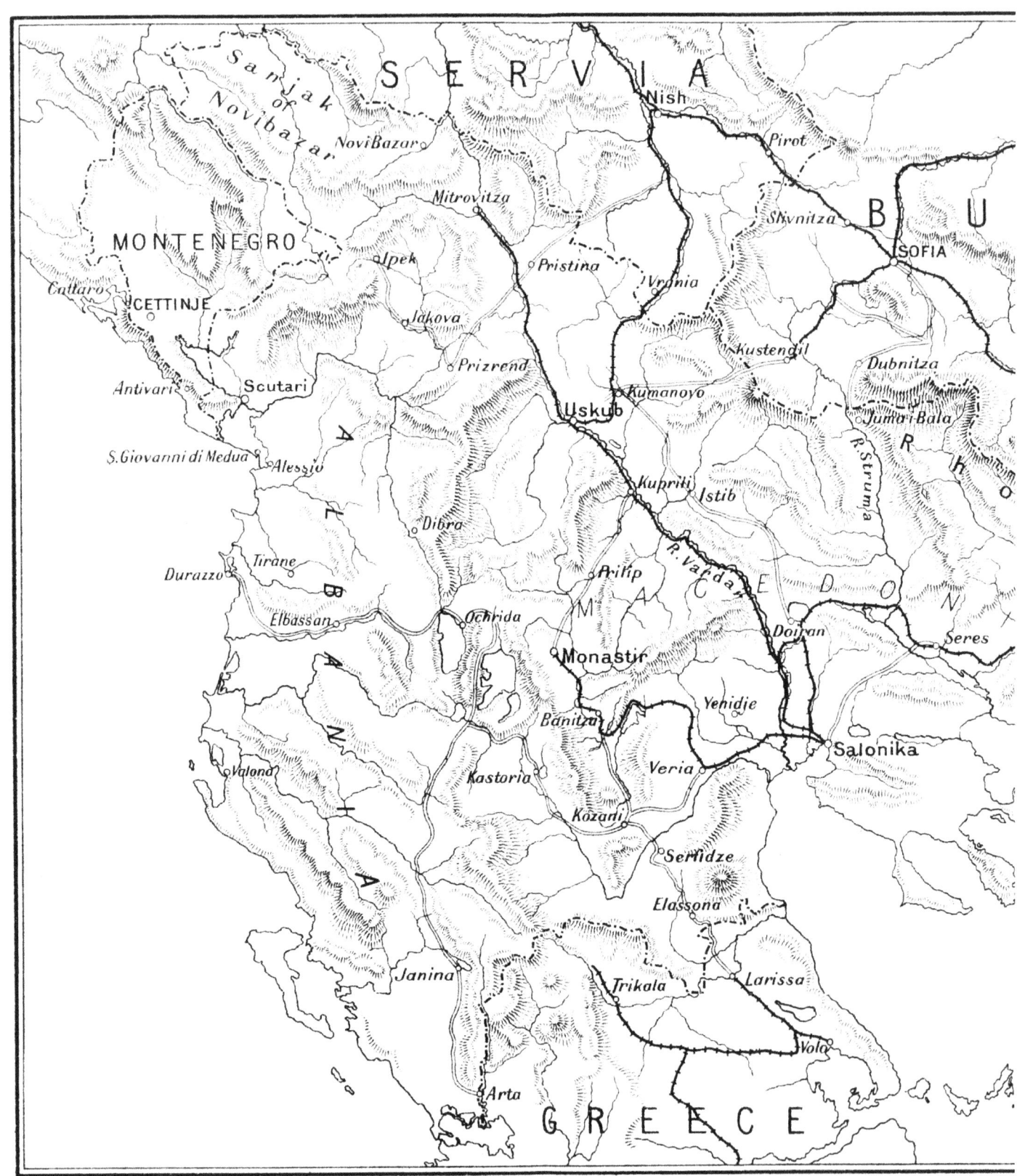

PREFACE

THE following six lectures were given, more or less in the form they are now printed, at the Staff College, Camberley, in February and March, 1913, after a visit to the Headquarters of the Bulgarian Army in the field and to the battlefields of Thrace, during the armistice, between the first and second phases of the war. At the request of the G.O.C.-in-Chief, Sir Douglas Haig, four of the lectures were afterwards repeated to officers of the Aldershot Command.

My visit was neither to strangers nor to a strange land. For my earliest friendships with Bulgarian officers date from 1903; and during four previous visits to the Balkans I had already travelled over practically the whole of the area with which my lectures deal.

I take this opportunity to thank Lieutenant-General Savoff, Major-General Fitcheff and the officers of the Headquarter Staff for their great kindness and hospitality throughout my visit, and for their readiness to disclose and discuss much which till then had remained secret with regard to the operations of the Bulgarian armies in Thrace.

I owe special acknowledgment to Major Bakargieff, of the Operations Section of the General Staff at Headquarters, who conducted me round the battlefields; to Colonel Jostoff, Chief of the Staff of the Third Army, and of the combined Third and First Armies whenever the combination was effected, who took infinite trouble in explaining to me details of the work of these two armies; and to Captain Stefanoff, of the Intelligence Section of the General Staff of the Second Army, who described to me the operations of the Second Army round Adrianople.

I feel convinced that all did their best to furnish me with a frank, though always very modest, account of their own experiences in the field, and with an accurate outline of the course of the campaign up to the end of the battle of Lule Burgas-Bunar Hissar. That was all for which I asked. As the Tchatalja operations were unfinished at the time of my visit, disclosures and discussions about them could hardly be expected; and in any case their strategical and tactical interest is comparatively small.

I must, however, lay stress upon two possible sources of error with regard to all details mentioned in my lectures. In the first place it is a principle of the Bulgarian General Staff always to be looking to the future and to let the past look after itself. My informants were therefore

PREFACE vii

careful to impress upon me that accuracy of detail could not be guaranteed, and that much which they told me might be subject to revision when the official records were eventually checked and compiled. Secondly, I have had to trust largely to my memory, for it was impossible to note down at once everything heard in the course of numerous conversations; and, in any case, midwinter conditions in Thrace were not conducive to much writing.

An official history of the war will, I understand, be put in hand by the Bulgarian General Staff as soon as peace is signed, but whether that history will ever be published outside Bulgaria remains to be seen.

I am indebted to the Editor of *The Times* for permission to quote extracts from six articles, which I wrote on my return for that paper, and for leave to reproduce some of the maps used to illustrate those articles.

All maps of Thrace are based upon a very rough survey made by the Russians during their temporary occupation of Turkish territory at the end of the Russo-Turkish war of 1877. All are therefore inaccurate; but the best, as the Bulgarians themselves were ready to acknowledge, is the $\frac{1}{250,000}$ map prepared by the Geographical Section of the General Staff at the War Office, London.

The spelling of place names on this War Office map does not, however, always agree with that employed in *The Times*. I have adhered to the latter in order to make my text as far as possible agree with my maps.

PHILIP HOWELL,
Major,
General Staff.

STAFF COLLEGE,
CAMBERLEY,
May 15, 1913.

Contents

FIRST LECTURE

	PAGE
PREPARATIONS AND PLANS	1

Initiative in War: General Plan of Campaign: Plan of Invasion of Thrace.

SECOND LECTURE

MOBILIZATION AND CONCENTRATION 25

Protection of the Frontier: Measures to Mislead the Turks: Organization and Command of the Bulgarian Armies: Employment of the Cavalry Division.

THIRD LECTURE

STRATEGICAL DEPLOYMENT, 18TH–21ST OCTOBER . . 42

Supposed Turkish Dispositions: Declaration of War: Advance of the Second Army: Advance of the Third Army: Employment of the Cavalry Division.

FOURTH LECTURE

BATTLES OF 22ND–23RD OCTOBER 60

Dispositions on evening of 21st October: Battle of Seliolu: Battle of Petra-Erikler: Capture of Kirk Kilisse: Battles of Kaipa and Yurush: Situation at Headquarters: Turkish Movements.

CONTENTS

FIFTH LECTURE

BATTLE OF LULE BURGAS–BUNAR HISSAR . . . 85

Dispositions on evening of 24th October: the Cavalry Reconnaissance: Plan of Attack: Measures to Mislead the Turks: System of Command: The Advance: Fighting on the First Day, 28th October: The Second Day, 29th October: Frontal Attack by Third Army: Action of the Commanders: The Sortie from Adrianople: The Third Day, 30th October: The Fourth Day, 31st October: The Fifth Day, 1st November: Employment of the Cavalry Division: Failure of the General Plan and of the Pursuit.

SIXTH LECTURE

NOTES AND COMMENTS 139

Special Value of the War: A War with Ill-trained Forces: A Colonial War: The Fog of War: Art of Command: Development of the Bulgarian Army and its General Staff: Moral and Psychological Considerations: Use of the Bayonet: Evening Attacks: Armament and Equipment: Entrenchments.

MAPS

GENERAL MAP of the Balkan Peninsula . *At beginning*

MAP No. 1. Peace disposition of the Bulgarian Divisions. . . . *Facing page* 40

MAP No. 2. Concentrations of the Bulgarian Armies and supposed Concentrations of the Turks . . . . . ,, ,, 98

MAP No. 3. Northern Thrace, showing the battles of 22nd-23rd October . ,, ,, 84

MAP No. 4. Battle of Lule Burgas–Bunar Hissar . . . . . . ,, ,, 138

MAP No. 5. To illustrate the operations of the Second Army around Adrianople . *At end*

FIRST LECTURE

PRELIMINARY PREPARATIONS AND PLANS

MAPS.—General (at beginning) and No. 1, (page 40).

"FOOLS," wrote Bismarck, "say that you can gain experience only at your own expense, but I have always contrived to gain my experience at the expense of others." Bismarck's opinion on this point should be particularly encouraging to the soldier who strives in peace to prepare himself for war. Because for him experience at the expense of others is essential; experience at his own expense he cannot get; the soldier in peace must profit by the experience of the soldier in war, or profit not at all.

To talk of practical as opposed to theoretical peace training is to draw a distinction which in reality hardly exists, for in peace all training must be more or less theoretical. Tactical training, for instance, must always be based upon a theoretical state of war and be dependent very largely on imagination. The more closely, then, we can in imagination share the experiences which others have gained in practice, the greater our probable profit.

To do so, do we require a complete and accurate record of the war in which they fought, and of all its kaleidoscopic changes, hour by hour or day by day ?

I think not. For no soldiers engaged in war are ever in possession of a complete and accurate record of its details. On the contrary they are always wondering what has happened, and what will happen next; full knowledge of the situation as a whole at any given moment is the last thing they ever attain.

If, then, we are to share their experiences, we must share not only their knowledge but also their *ignorance*, both of past and of coming events. We must try to see the problems as they were seen by those who had to face them ; to grasp not what happened but what was expected to happen ; what was attempted and how ; which attempts succeeded and which attempts failed; and what were the causes of these successes and failures.

Lastly, in order to gain practice, in order to profit without paying the price, we must not only try to see the problems as they really were, but we must also try to solve them ; to think them out and then decide what, in similar circumstances, we should have done ourselves. Thought without decision is of little practical value in military affairs.

* * * * *

It is with these principles in view that I shall try to approach this campaign in Thrace. My lectures will deal only with the opening phase, up to and including the battle of Lule Burgas—Bunar Hissar, a period of three weeks of actual war. And they will deal with it from only one point of view, that of the Bulgarian commanders and their staffs. My object will be to put before you not a mere narrative of events but rather a series of problems, each as it appeared to Bulgarian headquarters at the time.

In neither accuracy nor inaccuracy will my data for each problem ever quite correspond to the data possessed by the Bulgarian General Staff. I do not profess to know all the secrets of the latter, nor to be able to paint the problems exactly as they were. I aim only at sufficient resemblance to make their study worth consideration.

The difficulty and the danger of drawing conclusions from data neither accurate nor complete must be obvious to all. The lessons must therefore be taken for what they are worth—and no more.

* *

*

The Initiative in War.

The agreement between Bulgaria and Servia was signed in March 1912; that between Bulgaria and the other allies, Greece and Montenegro, within the next two months. Thus the alliance was completed by May.

Now, whatever the terms in which these agreements were cloaked, the alliance meant an aggressive policy; and an aggressive policy meant war.

An aggressive, or offensive war.

From the moment the league was formed the initiative, from both the political and the military standpoint, lay with the Allies. They could select the season which suited them best for the commencement of hostilities; and, by keeping their compact secret and avoiding an open quarrel until that right moment arrived, they could probably begin their war by surprise. Turkey could thus be surprised and thrown upon the defensive at the outset. And, even if the secrets of the alliance and its objects became known, Turkey, it was obvious, would be unlikely to take the offensive; for, being already at war with Italy, she would hesitate to attack four other States and so become involved with five.

The initiative, then, lay with the Allies in the sense that they could choose their time; but it lay with them in yet another sense.

The two initial steps in any war are, first, mobilization—the change from peace to war footing—and, next, concentration in the sphere of operations; and the side which completes these preliminary phases first is in a position to assume the offensive, to pipe the tune to which the other must dance.

Now the rate at which these two steps can be completed depends upon organization; upon the rapidity with which instructions reach reservists and the latter reach their depôts; upon the distances to be covered from mobilization centres to points of concentration; and upon the internal communications, of which, of course, the most important are railways. Obviously in these respects the advantage lay with the Allies, whose organization was better, and in whose countries

PREPARATIONS AND PLANS

distances were less and railway communications more highly developed.

* * * * *

FIRST PROBLEM. Accordingly, one of the first problems calling for solution by the allied general staffs was the selection of the most propitious date; the decision when to begin.

We all know the overwhelming advantages of the initiative; of waging war offensively. How were these advantages to be best utilized? The answer to this question involved the mature consideration of very many points.

The adversary, Turkey, was already at war with Italy and steadily going down hill; losing in prestige and in morale; losing financially, because trade was suffering and because an abnormal number of men were being kept under arms. Turkey, moreover, was in difficulties in other ways; political parties were at daggers drawn; dissensions were rife in the army; rebellions in progress in Albania and Arabia; a boycott in force against Greece.

Amongst the Allies, on the other hand, things were on the upward grade; progress was being made. For instance, Greece, though unready, was rapidly re-organizing both her army and her fleet. In Bulgaria itself certain military measures awaited completion, including the trans-Balkan railway running from Tirnovo to Stara Zagora, important both for mobilization purposes and as a line of supply.

Note, in passing, that war preparations of this nature must be completed in peace as a rule, if they are to be completed at all, for the outbreak of war, of a big war, means dislocation everywhere. Armies and navies can seldom be successfully reorganized during war; or railways or battleships built, once war has been declared. Economists may argue that they can, but history tends to show that they can not. Take as two instances the very two matters mentioned above. The reorganization of the Greek army was incomplete when war was declared; and to lack of organization may be traced its inability to play any prominent rôle during the early and decisive phases of the war. Whilst, although only a mile or two of the Tirnovo-Stara Zagora railway remained unfinished when mobilization began, the connexion, in spite of its military importance, has not even yet been made (March 1913).

With things going badly in Turkey and well amongst the Allies there was no necessity to hurry on the war. Delay was not disadvantageous. The general staffs could afford to await the most suitable season of the year. When would that be?

* * * * *

A national war, war waged by a nation in arms, means national stagnation, more or less; an end to all trade, commerce and production.

Therefore, finish it as rapidly as possible; and therefore, also, select the season in which the pinch will be least felt.

In an agricultural country the slack season is well defined, after the autumn harvest. The harvest ended, the farmer, the agricultural labourer, their horses and their oxen, are for a period free

PREPARATIONS AND PLANS

—this being one of the many military advantages of the agricultural as opposed to the industrial state. In Bulgaria the harvest is over and the vineyards are plucked by the end of September.

Again, the Bulgarian soldier commences his course with the colours—nominally a two years' course, in practice rather less—in February, and completes it in October.

The peace establishment army is therefore at its best, the nucleus of the war army is in its most efficient state, in the autumn.

Again, a winter campaign in the Balkans hits the men hard; but it was likely to hit the Turk harder than the Bulgar. In winter troops are called upon to fight both the elements and the enemy; and success in the former struggle depends upon organization and physique. Bulgarian organization was likely to prove superior to Turkish, for winter manœuvres had long been a regular feature in the Bulgarian training programme.

Again, physical development claims great attention in the Bulgarian army and schools; and the average Bulgar, soldier or civilian, is harder, more muscular and more accustomed to long hours of outdoor labour, than is the less industrious, happy-go-lucky, coffee-drinking Turk —especially the Turk from Anatolia, or from still more eastern or southern, and therefore still warmer, climes.

Further, in the summer and early autumn the heat in the Macedonian valleys and in Thrace is great, and the water supply is scarce.

Lastly, war in the autumn would probably be

less expected by the outside world, and would come more as a surprise to the Turks. It is the spring rather than the autumn, the time when the snow begins to melt rather than when it begins to fall, which has usually heralded disturbances in south-eastern Europe; "trouble in the Balkans in the spring" is an expression which all have often heard.

* * * * *

On the whole, then, the autumn seemed to Bulgaria the most suitable season to select for the opening of the war. And it was eventually decided that mobilization should begin at the end of September.

The alliance itself and the decision of the Allies to take the offensive in the autumn were kept secret; with such success that just before the quarrel was finally picked Turkey discharged a large contingent of soldiers from the active list to the reserve.

In view of the vast interests involved, the maintenance of these secrets,—the secret of the alliance, the secret of the decision to attack, and the secret of the selection of the most favourable time—forms in each case a lesson in itself.

For instance, if any foreign general staff should happen to contemplate offensive action against the British Empire, that offensive action would probably begin not when our navy and its personnel were all prepared; when our command of the sea was assured; when the regular and territorial forces were up to strength, fully trained and ready either to embark or to take the field at home.

That, at least, is not the time to expect offensive action if foreign staffs have profited by this first lesson of the Balkan war.

* * * * *

By the autumn Bulgarian preparations were so well advanced that time was found to carry out some preliminary peace manœuvres. The plan of operations as a whole could not be practised without giving its secrets away, but one portion of it, the investment of a fortress, was rehearsed—Shumla being made to play the part of Adrianople; and for this purpose two divisions, most of the cavalry, and all the army staffs were mobilized.

Preparations need to be very complete to enable action of this sort to be taken just prior to a war. Imagine, for instance, the staffs of our War Office and Aldershot Command manœuvring in Ireland a fortnight before embarking at Southampton for important operations over sea.

* *

*

THE GENERAL PLAN OF CAMPAIGN.

So much for the first problem, the selection of the season of the year.

Having decided that question, the Bulgarian general staff had next to consider the plan of operations as a whole—Bulgaria's best rôle as one of the four Allied States.

SECOND PROBLEM.

Now the first common object of the Allies was to drive the Turks out of European Turkey. And, with the former enjoying the advantages of a better organization, of greater readiness for war, of the selection of the moment for opening hostilities, of the initiative from the outset, and of a preliminary superiority in numbers when combined, this first object seemed attainable with comparative ease.

The second object of the Allies was to hit the Turks so hard that, having lost their European provinces, they would accept the loss and agree to terms of peace; and agree quickly—because the longer the war the greater the cost, the greater the drain upon limited resources. Bearing in mind the character of the Turk, this second object was likely to prove more difficult, and might require nothing short of the occupation of Constantinople.

This eventuality must have been fully realized before the war began. There can be no limited liability in war, and those who go to war at all must always be prepared to see the matter through. It is not always sufficient to beat the enemy's armies in the field, or to sink his ships. It may often be necessary to take a further step and lay hands, for instance, upon some vital spot. Capitals are not necessarily vital spots. But the possession of Constantinople is probably vital to the Turkish Empire, at any rate to the Turkish Empire of 1912. In much the same way London is probably vital to the British Empire, a consideration that any one going to war with Great Britain would be sure to bear in mind.

These, then, were the two primary objectives of the Allies—to drive the Turks out of Europe,

PREPARATIONS AND PLANS 11

and to keep them out by obtaining, quickly, suitable terms of peace.

The secondary objective of each ally—Bulgaria of course included—was to peg out the largest possible claim for itself.

What would be Bulgaria's best policy to attain these different ends ?

* * * * *

The lie of the land and the normal distribution of the Turkish troops in peace divided the theatre of operations into two areas, Macedonia and Thrace. (*See* General Map.)

Now in Thrace the situation of the Turks was strategically strong.

A defensible frontier, protected by the neighbouring hills and by the garrisons and works of Adrianople and Kirk Kilisse. The flanks secure ; the one resting on the Istranja Mountains and the Black Sea, a sea commanded by the Turks ; the other resting on obstacles, the Rhodope Mountains and the Maritza river. The bases, Constantinople, Rodosto and other ports along the coast of the Marmora, equally secure. Safe communications by rail and by sea with these bases, and with the Asiatic provinces and all their vast resources in men, animals and supplies.

In Macedonia the situation of the Turks was strategically weak.

The armies of the Allies surrounded them on almost every side. The chief land communication between the eastern and the western areas, the Dedeagatch-Salonica railway, was exposed throughout its course to raids by either land or sea.

The main base was Salonica—the principal port of Macedonia and the point where the only three railways meet. But Salonica was a port and nothing else, and a seaport forms a suitable base only if command of the adjacent sea is assured. If not assured, as well be based upon a desert. Italy, being in control of the Aegean Sea, made this main base, Salonica, so insecure as to be a base only in name, for she interfered with all mobilization arrangements and with the transport of reinforcements and supplies. Moreover, should the Italians make peace there was a strong probability that the Greeks would take their place and would acquire at least partial command of the sea,—would seriously threaten the sea passages, if unable to control them altogether.

* * * * *

For Bulgaria there was another and quite distinct consideration, the attitude of Roumania. Whatever Bulgarian politicians might think or say; whatever guarantees Roumania herself might give; or whatever guarantees great Powers might give on Roumania's behalf—the danger of Roumanian interference was always there. There was the possibility of some understanding between Roumania and Turkey. Roumania was one of the Balkan States, but not a member of the Balkan League; and she stood to lose more than she stood to gain should the latter prove successful in its enterprises.

Strategically, however, she could threaten Bulgaria alone, not the other Allies.

By a stretch of imagination the Roumanian

PREPARATIONS AND PLANS

question for Bulgaria may be compared with what in India is known as the problem of internal defence, i.e. the protection of India from possible dangers within its borders should its army ever be engaged without.

* * * * *

Bulgaria had also to remember the possibility of defection amongst her allies. The friendship amongst them was barely skin deep, and, although their interests were in common on the greater issues of the war, they were in conflict on its details. Moreover, the military reputations of these allies as they stood before the war did not inspire confidence; both Servians and Greeks had been the vanquished, not the victors, in most of their previous campaigns against the Turks.

A Bulgarian detachment to co-operate with them closely and set a good example might make much difference to their conduct.

* * * * *

Such being briefly the general situation, ought Bulgaria to leave Macedonia, where the Turks were comparatively weak, entirely to the other members of the league? Leave Macedonia to her allies, take all risks about Roumania, and concentrate every available man upon Thrace, where the Turks were comparatively strong?

Or should Bulgaria compromise? Place part of her forces in Macedonia, retain part to watch Roumania, and only put the balance into Thrace?

This problem deserves full consideration.

* * * * *

Strategically, the policy of concentration was in

all probability the boldest and the best. And in years to come Bulgaria's failure to adopt it is likely to be the criticism most freely and frequently applied to her general conduct of the war.

Bulgaria compromised.

The General Staff resolved to make two big detachments, the two together amounting to about one-sixth of the total available strength.

They decided to leave one division to act in the western or the weaker area, and to co-operate with the Servians and the Greeks. Thus it would cover the capital, Sofia, should things go wrong, or could peg out the Bulgarian claim to conquered territory should things go well.

They decided to employ another division in the Rhodope, between the western and the eastern areas, in order to guard their own railway communication along the Maritza valley, and to cut communication between the two main masses of the Turks by occupying points along the Dedeagatch-Salonica railway. Thence this detachment would turn east or west according to developments of the situation.

Lastly, they decided to take all risks about Roumania and to concentrate the remainder of their forces for the invasion of Thrace. And the problem which arises next is, how ? How invade Thrace ?

* *
*

PLAN OF INVASION OF THRACE.

All military operations are to a certain extent dictated by topography; and the Bulgarian

PREPARATIONS AND PLANS

General Staff were, of course, familiar with the topographical features of Thrace.

Thrace, or more properly speaking the Turkish *vilayat*, or province, of Adrianople, is about the size of Yorkshire. Its approximate boundaries have already been mentioned. On the west lies the Rhodope Balkan, of which the main backbone ends more or less abruptly in the Maritza valley, some six miles west of Mustafa Pasha. The spur which runs down from this point to the junction of the Arda and Maritza rivers, and the irregular chains of minor mountains lying west of the lower Maritza—the river below Adrianople —and between the Arda and the sea are difficult, but not impassable, for armies on the march. Not, indeed, as difficult as the hachuring or contours on most maps make them seem to be; not nearly as difficult, for instance, as the Motienling mountains, through which Kuroki's army marched and manœuvred in 1904. Still, roadless; the slopes in places fairly steep; and the valleys deep and boggy after rain. The greater part of what is coloured green and labelled forest on our $\frac{1}{250,000}$ General Staff (War Office) map is little more than scrub.

North of Mustafa Pasha, where the frontier makes its bend, is a clump of comparatively high hills, the Sakar Planina, lying between the Maritza and the Tundja valleys. From the Tundja river eastwards the frontier follows the watershed as far as the Black Sea, but not until the Istranja Balkan begins to be reached, in the neighbourhood of Kaibilar, do these frontier hills form very serious obstacles to troops, except that there are no roads.

16 THE CAMPAIGN IN THRACE

Once across the frontier and a few miles south of the watershed, natural obstacles practically cease; the country between the lower Maritza and the western slopes of the Istranja becomes open, rolling down-land, and so it continues all the way south to the sea.

The Maritza, the Tundja and the Arda rivers are considerable obstacles; the first, below Adrianople, being about as wide and deep as the lower reaches of the Thames; the last two about as big as the Thames at Windsor. All three are in winter very liable to flood, and bridges are few and far between.

The land is practically undeveloped and therefore poor; not that the soil is barren or Nature unkind, but that the country is thinly populated, and where there are few cultivators the crops must obviously be small. Moreover, during the long years of Turkish maladministration, there have been few markets, great difficulties of intercourse and transport, little or no security. The inhabitants have therefore been accustomed to sow just enough to satisfy their own requirements and those of the Turkish tax collectors, and no more. Except, then, that after the autumn harvest stores laid in for winter consumption might be commandeered, there is normally no surplus, nothing to spare for either invading or defending armies. The Bulgarians, therefore, could rely upon finding very little; their troops would have to carry all, or nearly all, their own supplies. That meant, of course, abnormal strain upon, abnormal importance of, communications—the roads and railways.

PREPARATIONS AND PLANS

Only one railway and only one metalled road crosses the frontier between Bulgaria and Thrace, and both these follow the Maritza valley; elsewhere what on maps are sometimes shown as roads are merely tracks.

* * * * *

Equally well known to the Bulgarian General Staff must have been the normal distribution of the Turkish troops in Thrace.

These forces included the nucleus of four army corps with headquarters at Constantinople, Rodosto, Kirk Kilisse and Adrianople respectively. Each corps consisted of three divisions of *nizam* and had an indefinite peace establishment, averaging perhaps 10,000 men, and a theoretical war establishment of roughly 30,000. Note that a Turkish division is roughly the equivalent of a Bulgarian brigade; and a Turkish corps roughly the equivalent of a Bulgarian division. It was known, however, that one division of the Ist Corps (Constantinople) had been sent away to Albania; and that the headquarters of one division of the IInd Corps (Rodosto) were in time of peace at Smyrna. In addition were the cadres of five divisions of *redif*; and the fortress troops of Adrianople, roughly the equivalent of another army corps. Total available in Thrace, excluding fortress troops:—

10 divisions of *nizam*,
5 ,, ,, *redif*,

with a war strength of, say, 150,000.

How quickly these European units could be raised from peace to war strength by the enrolment of recruits from the local population, and by the recall of reservists from Asia Minor; and how quickly Asiatic units could be imported to reinforce those in Thrace were questions which could not be answered with any certainty. Calculations were further complicated, firstly, by the more than usual irregularity of strengths and dispositions which internal disorders and the existing state of war (with Italy) had brought about; and secondly, by the fact that the organization of the Turkish army as a whole, an organization which at its best had existed but on paper, was in process of transition—at any rate in theory.

At what conclusions the Bulgarian General Staff were able to arrive I do not know. But as a basis for study let us assume that they calculated on 100,000 armed men being present in Thrace before a Turkish mobilization was officially decreed: and that they estimated that these numbers could be raised to 200,000 by the time the Bulgarian mobilization was completed.

We must remember, however, that the completion of mobilization in Bulgaria meant the absorption of practically all men capable of bearing arms; whereas the gradual expansion of the Turkish forces could continue for many weeks, or even months.

* * * * *

The headquarters of the nine divisions into

PREPARATIONS AND PLANS

which the Bulgarian army is divided in peace are shown on Map No. 1., viz. :—

1st Division	at	Sofia
2nd ,,	,,	Philippopolis
3rd ,,	,,	Sliven
4th ,,	,,	Shumla
5th ,,	,,	Rustchuk
6th ,,	,,	Vratza
7th ,,	,,	Dubnitza
8th ,,	,,	Stara Zagora.
9th ,,	,,	Plevna

After deducting two divisions for the detachments mentioned on page 14 there remained for the invasion of Thrace seven, plus two extra divisions, the 10th and 11th, which were to be raised on the outbreak of war. Total, nine divisions.

THIRD PROBLEM. Bearing in mind the conditions mentioned above, how could these nine divisions, destined for the invasion of Thrace, be best employed?

That is my third problem. There are several alternative solutions, and they are all worth thinking out.

* * * * *

The natural and historical lines of invasion from Bulgaria into Thrace are, of course, along the Maritza and the Tundja valleys.

Both these were blocked by the fortress of Adrianople.

Therefore, whatever the plan for the invasion of Thrace, Adrianople stood most inconveniently in the way. Moreover, the Turks were almost certain to do as they did, that is to leave a large mobile garrison under cover of the Adrianople forts.

A garrison of this sort could not be ignored. The Bulgarians invading Thrace might perhaps avoid the fortress, but they could not pass it by and leave its garrison free to play havoc with their flanks and rear.

Adrianople, therefore, must either be attacked or masked; that much was obvious.

One alternative, then, was to make Adrianople the first objective; to attack it with the idea of carrying the attack right home; to capture it and so open the main lines of invasion before attempting any further move.

Now a first class fortress can rarely be rushed —as Nogi, for instance, learnt when he tried to rush Port Arthur and failed, with a loss of 14,000 men. The attack and capture of a fortress are far more likely to prove both costly and slow. But Bulgaria could afford to lose neither men nor time. Campaigns are won not by capturing fortresses, as a rule, but by defeating the enemy's main masses in the field; and the more men Bulgaria lost, and the more time she lost, the greater would be the numerical superiority of the Turks when eventually that main battle came to be fought.

If Adrianople could neither be ignored nor yet attacked, only one course remained—namely, to mask or contain the fortress and its garrison.

To mask may often mean to attack, but to attack in a modified sense; to attack with the idea of keeping the enemy tied to his trenches,

PREPARATIONS AND PLANS

rather than to attack with the idea of turning him out of them.

Assuming a decision to mask Adrianople with a detachment, the question next arises by which route, or routes, should the main mass enter Thrace? Past the east or west of Adrianople, or simultaneously past both sides?

The choice of routes depends primarily on the objective; that is to say, the road is more often dictated by the destination than the destination by the road.

What was the objective of the main Bulgarian mass? Obviously the main Turkish mass, and the more rapidly the latter could be reached and struck the better. Where exactly that would be, what area the Turks would select for their main concentration, no one in Bulgaria could with certainty foretell. But it would be likely to be somewhere in the centre of Thrace; somewhere where the pivots, Adrianople and Kirk Kilisse, would be covering more or less the front, and the obstacles, the Maritza river and the Istranja mountains, covering more or less the flanks; somewhere, too, within easy reach of the main Constantinople-Adrianople railway.

At any rate, wherever the main Turkish mass might be, a Bulgarian advance into the centre of Thrace would be likely to attract it magnetically and so to bring about the desired battle.

To divide the main Bulgarian mass in two and to attempt to pass Adrianople on both sides have obvious disadvantages.

An invasion past the *west* and south of Adrianople was probably not impossible, starting from about Hebibtchevo, for instance, in the Maritza valley and directed upon Demotika, as a first objective; thence to turn east. But such an advance would be through rough and hilly country; it would involve the passage of two rivers; and, confined between the Maritza and the Rhodope, the armies would find but little space for manœuvre.

Again, Hebibtchevo is further from Mandra than any point on the frontier to the north-east of Adrianople, and operations directed generally on Mandra, a railway junction and the central point of Thrace, were the most likely means of bringing the Turks to decisive battle.

Lastly, an advance on Mandra past Demotika would probably mean meeting the Turks at right angles to, and covering, their main line of communication, the railway to Constantinople; so that a victory would be less decisive—the Turks would be driven back along this line instead of off it.

The third possibility was to pass by the *east* of Adrianople; to march parallel to the Tundja valley and leave the fortress on the west.

Any advance along this line would raise at once the question of Kirk Kilisse. Kirk Kilisse was known to be the peace headquarters of a Turkish army corps, a cavalry brigade and certain army troops; and to be a strong natural position, protected by two permanent forts and easily made stronger by temporary field works. Its strategical importance was so fully recognized in Turkey

PREPARATIONS AND PLANS

that a railway had recently been constructed to connect it with the main line at Mandra. Kirk Kilisse was likely to be held, and held in force: and, like Adrianople, Kirk Kilisse could not be ignored by the invaders. Should Kirk Kilisse be attacked or masked?

The disadvantages of attacking Kirk Kilisse are similar to the disadvantages of attacking Adrianople, but of course in a less degree. On the other hand, to attempt to mask both Adrianople and Kirk Kilisse would mean two strong detachments and a great reduction of the Bulgarian mass destined to meet the Turkish mass, wherever that might be. Adrianople is but thirty miles from Kirk Kilisse, and to mask these two places and advance through the narrow gap between them would be a risky operation; whilst an advance past the outer flank, to the east of Kirk Kilisse, was barred by the Istranja Balkan.

The Bulgarian General Staff decided that Kirk Kilisse must be taken.

* * * * *

Thus, the plan for the invasion of Thrace was briefly as follows:—

Firstly, as quickly as possible to surround and mask the fortress of Adrianople, devoting to this purpose not more than the necessary minimum of troops;

Secondly, to attack and take Kirk Kilisse;

Thirdly, with the troops who had stormed Kirk Kilisse and with every possible man who could be spared from the masking operations around Adrianople, to meet the Turkish mass, wherever that might be by the time these preliminary measures were completed.

Such were the general idea and the series of objectives up to the first encounter between the two main bodies; and to attempt to look very far beyond that point is seldom wise in war.

* *

*

SECOND LECTURE

MOBILIZATION AND CONCENTRATION

MAPS:—No. 1. (page 40). No. 2. (page 98).

ONCE the date upon which mobilization could most advantageously begin, and the general plan had been decided, it remained for the Foreign Office to defer a diplomatic crisis until the right season arrived, and for the War Office then to put the plan into execution.

Now it has already been shown that several alternative plans of campaign were open to the Bulgarians. Such a situation has the great advantage that it is possible to mislead the enemy into expecting attack from any but the real quarter.

Consequently the next problem for the Bulgarian General Staff involved two considerations, viz. :—

FOURTH PROBLEM. to mobilize and concentrate in such a way (a) that the selected plan could be carried out; and (b) that the enemy would expect not the real plan but another; that is to bring off a strategical surprise.

It is hard enough to bring off tactical surprises with companies and squadrons. How then are strategical surprises with whole armies to be effected? How concentrate nine whole divisions, each 20,000–30,000 strong, on the frontier of

Thrace in such a way as to be able rapidly to mask Adrianople; and in such a way as to be able to develop a surprise attack upon Kirk Kilisse?

That is my fourth problem.

* * * * *

Mobilization of the Bulgarian army began on the 30th September. This fact could not be concealed for long because under modern conditions, and when national armies are concerned, there can be no great mystery about actual mobilization; the secret must almost certainly leak out as soon as reservists begin to join their depôts—as soon as all normal business ceases and the whole manhood of a nation puts on the garb of war. But the news of internal movements and concentrations can be suppressed, and stories of false ones can be circulated.

Accordingly, the first steps to be taken were to institute a very rigid censorship, and a close blockade along the frontiers.

For the latter purpose sixteen frontier companies formed part of the military organization in peace, but these were insufficient to protect the 400 miles of Turkish frontier; reinforcements were required at once. Not only was it necessary to shut out spies and small patrols, but some danger existed of Turkish troops crossing the frontier in force and interfering seriously with warlike preparations. For, in the first place, the headquarters of the Turkish IIIrd and IVth Army Corps were at Kirk Kilisse and Adrianople respectively, and therefore close to the northern frontier of Thrace. And in the second, the Turks were known to possess

MOBILIZATION AND CONCENTRATION 27

a very marked superiority in mounted troops, the Thracian group of army corps alone being credited with five cavalry brigades, or roughly 8,000 sabres.

What proportion of these northern corps and mounted troops were actually ready at the end of September for immediate action was not known; but autumn manœuvres by Turkish troops in northern Thrace had been under discussion for some time, and it was possible that advantage had been taken of this fact to bring a proportion of the units up to war strength before mobilization had been publicly decreed. In any case, an invasion of Bulgaria by hordes of Turkish cavalry as the first act in any Turkish plan of campaign had been talked about for many years, and the Bulgarian General Staff was therefore compelled to pay some attention to these threats.

Two special measures were taken to guard against the risk.

The peace and war establishments of the Bulgarian cavalry regiments are practically the same; that is to say, their mobilization is a very simple process. Of the eleven available regiments all except one, left with the 7th (Dubnitza) Division south of Sofia, were sent off early to the Thracian frontier; they actually started from their peace stations, or from where they had been manœuvring round Shumla, a few days before the general mobilization began. On reaching the frontier these ten regiments were formed into a division of some 24 squadrons, or about 3,500 men, under Major-General Nazlumoff, the Inspector of Cavalry, and a brigade of 9 squadrons under Colonel Taneff—the former to watch the main approaches from Kirk Kilisse and the north of Adrianople, with its headquarters at Kizil Agatch in the Tundja valley; the latter to watch the Maritza valley and vicinity, with headquarters at Hebibtchevo.

Next, this protective line was lengthened and strengthened by three of the southern divisions, the 7th (Dubnitza) occupying the frontier passes south of Sofia, the 2nd (Philippopolis) the line of the Rhodope, and the 3rd (Sliven) supporting the cavalry division in the Tundja valley. The necessity to establish strong covering forces on the frontier directly war became imminent had been recognized beforehand; and the mobilization arrangements of these southern divisions had been so accelerated that complete units could be collected, equipped and despatched within three days.

Thus within less than one week the frontier was adequately protected against any risk of Turkish raids, and behind the screen so formed the concentration of the main armies could proceed with safety.

*****

Establish censorship and block the frontier—these, then, were the first two steps taken with a view to mystify and mislead the Turks. But they were by no means the only measures.

As already mentioned, the nine divisions of the Bulgarian Army were disposed in peace as shown on Map No. 1; and were organized in three "in-

MOBILIZATION AND CONCENTRATION 29

spections." Although the statement had never, I believe, been officially published, the impression had been created that the divisions, as grouped in these peace "inspections," would in war form three armies under their three Inspectors-General, viz:—

a First, or Western, Army, consisting of the 1st (Sofia), 6th (Vratza), and 7th (Dubnitza) Divisions;

a Second, or Southern, Army, consisting of the 2nd (Philippopolis), 3rd (Sliven), and 8th (Stara Zagora) Divisions; and

a Third, or Northern, Army, consisting of the 4th (Shumla), 5th (Rustchuk), and 9th (Plevna) Divisions.

This organization would be known, of course, to the military authorities of Turkey; and upon it they would presumably base their estimate of the Bulgarian "order of battle." The peace grouping was, however, completely altered upon mobilization, and two new divisions were raised —measures in themselves likely seriously to upset the calculations of the Turkish General Staff. Because the value of information received about an enemy in war depends largely upon the correctness or otherwise of the original estimate made of his order of battle. If accurate, every little item fits into its place and tends to clear the situation; if inaccurate, each fresh item tends to make confusion worse confounded. Hence follows the importance of keeping army lists and mobilization tables, and the connection between them, strictly confidential in times of peace.

The 7th (Dubnitza) and 2nd (Philippopolis)

Divisions dropped out of the army formations altogether and became two independent divisions, destined to form the two detachments mentioned in the general plan and to operate in Macedonia and the Rhodope respectively.

The First Army was, then, composed of the 1st (Sofia), 3rd (Sliven), and the new 10th Division;

the Second Army of the 8th (Stara Zagora), 9th (Plevna), and the new 11th Division; and

the Third Army of the 4th (Shumla), 5th (Rustchuk), and 6th (Vratza) Divisions.

But until their journeys by road or by rail from peace stations to the respective areas of concentration were actually concluded not even the divisional commanders themselves knew to which army they had been allotted; and during their journeys units of the divisions were never aware of their destinations for more than one day ahead.

* * * * *

Two years ago autumn manœuvres were held in Turkey for the first time, and were carefully watched by the Bulgarian General Staff.

The general idea then was that Adrianople had been invested by a Blue (Bulgarian) army and that two hostile Blue masses were advancing upon Constantinople, the one passing Adrianople on the west, the other on the east, with the intention of uniting somewhere about the line Havsa-Demotika and of advancing thence against a Red (Turkish) army, which was concentrating to protect its capital in the neighbourhood of Lule Burgas. Abdulla Pasha commanded the Blue army on that occasion and Zekki Pasha (defeated by the Servians at Kumanovo) the Red.

There are, as already mentioned, several ways of invading Thrace; but, if you dismiss from your mind the possibility of any modern army with modern equipment making its way through the roadless and apparently impassable country lying between the Tundja valley and the Black Sea, Blue's strategy may appear the most obvious and the best. Anyhow, Marshal von der Goltz Pasha, who directed these manœuvres, and Mahmud Shevket Pasha, the Minister for War, seemed to be of this opinion, for they drew up the scheme and freely criticized its execution. The invaders were supposed to have had the best of the operations. So much so that, during the final battle which took place near Lule Burgas, in order to save the situation an imaginary army was suddenly made to appear from nowhere and dashed upon Abdulla Pasha's rear—for it would never have done to let a Turkish army be beaten by an invader, even at play! These manœuvres, being the first ever held, made a great sensation in Turkish military circles.

Now the Turk is essentially slow-witted, lacking in imagination and original ideas. It occurred to the Bulgarian General Staff that Abdulla Pasha, who when mobilization began was the senior officer in Thrace, might be induced to expect the Bulgarians from the direction in which Von der Goltz had made them appear; from the only direction, quite possibly, that Abdulla Pasha had ever seriously studied.

The deception was at least worth trying.

Accordingly, the Bulgarian Second Army was ordered to concentrate about Harmanli to correspond to the Blue army investing Adrianople in the manœuvre scheme; and the First Army to concentrate about Haskovo to form the Blue invading mass due to pass Adrianople on the west.

The concentration at Haskovo was, however, but a bogus one, carried out on paper only and arranged for the special benefit of the Turkish intelligence service, the war correspondents, and the foreign military attachés. The units of the First Army, including the 1st (Sofia) Division —the division at the capital, at the place where news would be most likely to get out—were duly ordered to Haskovo, but as each military train approached the railway station nearest to that point the troops were ordered to keep their seats and the journey was continued to Yamboli. The 3rd (Sliven) Division was, as narrated above, already in the Tundja valley, and in course of time the other two Divisions of the First Army—the 1st (Sofia) and the newly-raised 10th—found themselves there also, with army headquarters at Kizil Agatch.

Thus, the First Army during its concentration played a double rôle; it first acted the part of the western invading mass of the Turkish manœuvre scheme, and then became in reality the eastern.

Only one real, live brigade ever really reached Haskovo, and that was a brigade of the 2nd (Philippopolis) Division; which remained there until the advance began when it was attached to the Second Army, and with that army eventually took part in the investment of Adrianople.

MOBILIZATION AND CONCENTRATION 33

By about the time that the concentrations were completed—that is, by the middle of October—an intelligent observer with some knowledge of Bulgarian army organization, after sifting and compiling the various reports which must have been prevalent at this period, would be quite likely to arrive at the conclusion that one army was concentrating in the Tundja valley, one in the Maritza valley, and one further west. The last would extend perhaps from Haskovo to Dubnitza, but still, with a railway and good roads in its rear, would be able to concentrate to one flank or the other if required.

* * * * *

Meanwhile, where was the real Third Army? That was the great secret of the concentration, and so well was it kept that, when, if ever, a history of the campaign is written from the Turkish point of view, it will probably be found that the Turks at the outset were surprised—surprised at the rapidity with which the Bulgarian mobilization and concentration were completed, and surprised by the sudden appearance of a whole army of close upon 100,000 men from a totally unexpected direction.

As soon as the 3rd (Sliven) Division completed its mobilization and marched down south to support the cavalry division in the Tundja valley, the latter moved off further east and took up a protective line along the frontier from, roughly, Kaibilar to the Black Sea. Covered by the cavalry, and later by the First Army as the latter began to reach the vicinity of Kizil Agatch, the Third Army concentrated east of Yamboli with its headquarters about Straldja.

The 4th (Shumla) and 5th (Rustchuk) Divisions marched to this area, for the new railway from Tirnovo to Stara Zagora was not quite completed when the war began. The 6th (Vratza) Division was sent by rail round through Sofia ; and as far as Seimenli junction its unit commanders were under the delusion that they were on their way to join, not the Third, but the First Army about Haskovo, for in peace, as noted above, the 6th Division belongs to the First Inspection.

* *
*

ORGANIZATION AND COMMAND.

The 6th (Vratza) Division and the two new divisions, the 10th and 11th, were each composed of two brigades, the remainder all of three. In round numbers each brigade contained 10,000 fighting men, so that the total of the 30 brigades amounted roughly to 300,000 rifles.

Each of the divisions on the higher establishment included 9 quick-firing four-gun batteries and 6 six-gun batteries *à tir acceleré*. In the divisions on the lower establishment the artillery is in proportion, so that, including certain army units of howitzer and mountain artillery, the total number of field guns amounted roughly to 800.

The 11 regiments of cavalry counted 37 squadrons (4 regiments of 4 squadrons, 7 regiments of 3 squadrons), or about 5,500 sabres. Of these one regiment was allotted to each army, the army commander keeping as a rule about a half squadron in hand, dividing up the remainder to form divisional cavalry for his divisions. Each division had, in addition, a weak squadron of mounted gendarmes.

Excluding, then, the columns destined to operate in Macedonia, and excluding also the 11th Division, which was not fully mobilized until about a fortnight later, by the 17th October there were concentrated and ready for the invasion of Thrace three Bulgarian armies, amounting roughly to 230,000 rifles, 5,000 cavalry, and 600 guns.

* * * * *

General Headquarters assembled at Stara Zagora. The Commander-in-Chief was nominally the King, but executive command, with a very free hand, was delegated to the Assistant Commander-in-Chief, Lieutenant-General Michael Savoff. The chief of the staff was Major-General Fitcheff, who already held that post in peace.

The command of the three field armies was vested in the three Inspectors-General, Kutincheff, Ivanoff, and Radko Dimitrieff; with Colonels Papabapoff, Jaykoff, and Jostoff, the respective commandants of the Military School, the new Staff College, and the School for Reserve Officers, as chiefs of their staffs.

For about five years previous to the war General Savoff had, for political reasons, been living in retirement and had spent a great deal of that time abroad, in France. The question of supreme executive command in the event of war had frequently been raised in Bulgarian Government circles, but never fairly faced. When war became imminent one of the political parties had urged the appointment of a Council, on the grounds that the general plan of campaign involved problems too complicated and too vast to be within the capacity of one man to control. This proposal was quashed, with the full support of the Bulgarian General Staff, but the question remained unsettled. With the result that, when the crisis eventually, came the executive Commander-in-Chief was practically the only important individual who was called upon to assume an appointment for which he had not been previously warned, and who had therefore failed to get practice in his duties. Savoff, as a young captain, had commanded a wing of the Bulgarian army at the victory of Slivnitza in 1885. Since then he had in turn held all the high appointments in the Bulgarian army, including Minister of War and Chief of the General Staff. Therefore, whilst still a comparatively young man he had had exceptionally long experience in positions of responsibility and high command. Fitcheff and he were old friends, for when Savoff, ten to fifteen years ago, commanded the Military School the former had been his chief assistant. The combination of these two was said to be an admirable one—Savoff a man of great personality and determination, enjoying the full confidence of all ranks, ready always to accept responsibility, to take rapid decisions, and run necessary risks; Fitcheff a deep student, a master of detail, and blessed with a placid temperament enabling him to restrain on occasion the somewhat more impetuous disposition of his Chief.

MOBILIZATION AND CONCENTRATION 37

Bulgaria was fortunate in finding such a satisfactory solution of this question of supreme command.

But the fact that it had not been solved earlier, that such a vastly important point had been allowed to simmer unsettled, is acknowledged to have been a grave flaw in her military organization.

On the other hand, against all the obvious disadvantages of long absence from direct touch with the army one point was recognized to be an asset. Namely, that for five years Savoff, freed from all administrative duties, had had leisure to study his profession and think out quietly the bigger problems of modern war.

* *
*

Employment of the Cavalry Division.

During this period of mobilization and concentration, the cavalry, the most mobile troops, and those most readily raised from peace to war establishment, were employed to secure the frontier.

The cavalry division itself was first in the Tundja valley, where it covered the concentration of the First Army; and, when relieved by the outposts of the latter, it moved further east to cover the concentration of the Third Army.

Now the cavalry divisional commander, whilst carrying out these duties, was acting directly under the orders of the Commander-in-Chief, and sending copies only of his reports to the commanders of the First and Third Armies. So here was a cavalry division employed protectively, and yet carrying out a special, strategical mission, independently of the remainder of the force and directly under the orders of the Commander-in-Chief.

How should it be designated: " the independent cavalry " or " the protective mounted troops " ? (*See Field Service Regulations*, Part I, page 89.)

It might surely equally well be either ? That is a point worth noticing, because the tendency, during the last five or ten years, has been, perhaps, to carry to extremes the classification of cavalry and its duties; to try to divide the cavalry into " independent " and " protective," to draw hard and fast lines between them and to allot to each a quite distinct rôle.

This classification has its uses, but, if undue stress is laid upon it, it tends to become more confusing than advantageous. Adopted as a formula, it leads to the solution of problems upon preconceived ideas—the cavalry being employed to suit the regulations rather than the plan. In the long run, too, it is apt to obscure the main and practically the only point, namely, that the *same* man, or the same body of men—cavalry, infantry, or any other arm—cannot be expected *simultaneously* to carry out two *conflicting* missions. That is common sense. And if this truism is borne in mind there is no more necessity to talk of independent and protective cavalry than of independent and protective infantry or engineers.

Be that as it may, the classification breaks down

MOBILIZATION AND CONCENTRATION 39

in practice. For here is a cavalry division employed for the first time in war since these terms were introduced, into our own and other armies, and yet detailed straight away to carry out a mission which does not clearly fall under either heading—or falls equally well under both.

* * * * *

The handling of this Bulgarian cavalry division throughout the war is especially interesting to us for several reasons. Like the Bulgarians we have only one division, at any rate at present. Like them we shall have to make the most of it; and, like them, if we lose it, or wear it out, we shall have little to fall back upon. Moreover, it seems more likely than not that when we go to war it will be, as in their case, against an enemy possessing considerably more cavalry than do we. Accordingly, the detailed records of the Bulgarian cavalry division during the campaign in Thrace will be well worth studying when, if ever, they appear.

Its first mission was, then, to keep secret the concentration of the Third Army and to screen its eventual advance upon Kirk Kilisse; that is, to block the frontier and keep out spies and hostile patrols.

The cavalry could do this work best; and, provided that the duties involved were not too arduous, and did not involve undue wear and tear, the mission seems a very suitable one. Three weeks' quiet work patrolling the frontier; all ranks settling down in their saddles; horses getting fit and hard; men learning to fend for themselves; staffs and signal services obtaining plenty of real practice in that most difficult but most important duty, the maintenance of communication. There was no question of reconnaissance by the cavalry at this period, because war had not as yet been declared, and therefore the frontier could not be crossed by men in uniform.

* * * * *

Whilst on the subject of the employment of the cavalry at this stage there is one other point to note.

The cavalry division might be styled by those seeking to apply the spirit of our regulations, " the protective mounted troops "—protecting the Third Army. But it would be a mistake to suppose that the cavalry division was protecting the Third Army because the latter was incapable of protecting itself. Armies, divisions, brigades, all units must in war protect themselves. That is a very old-established rule. And the larger units in all military organizations are provided with a proportion of mounted troops —the divisional, or corps, or army cavalry— largely for this very purpose, to enable them to protect themselves. The larger they are the more warning they require, the more time to get ready to fight—unless already suitably disposed for action; and mounted men are therefore often indispensable, to give them timely warning.

The general principle, then, in our army, and the Bulgarian army, and every other army, is that all units must look after themselves. And the Third Army was just as capable of protecting itself as was the First Army, which at this period was not covered by the cavalry division. The

No 1

cavalry division, then, was disposed as it was not in order to relieve the Third Army of the responsibility of protecting itself; but for special and specific purposes that formed part of the general, strategical plan. These special purposes were to close down a portion of the frontier; to conceal the projected descent upon Kirk Kilisse; to mystify and mislead the enemy with regard to the strategical plan.

The points to grasp and note are, firstly, that normally all units must protect themselves in war. Secondly, that the cavalry of a force is a tool in the hands of the commander of that force, to be used not in accordance with any preconceived scheme or custom, as our regulations are a little inclined to imply, but elastically and in accordance with the requirements of the situation and the plan. And, when neither situation nor plan call for the employment of the cavalry, then the cavalry should rest, or march quietly forward, and not be wasted or worn out in the protection of other arms or units who can well protect themselves.

* *

*

THIRD LECTURE

THE STRATEGICAL DEPLOYMENT
18th.—21st. OCTOBER

MAPS.—No. 2, (page 98). No. 3, (page 84). No. 5, (at end).

BY the 17th October the Bulgarian forces were concentrated as follows:—

the Second Army (8th and 9th Divisions only —the 11th not yet being ready) in the Maritza valley,

the First Army (1st, 3rd and 10th Divisions) in the Tundja valley, and

the Third Army (4th, 5th and 6th Divisions) east of Yamboli, echelonned well back and covered partly by the First Army and partly by the cavalry division.

At Haskovo, away to the right of the Second Army but acting, I think, under its orders, was the brigade detached from the 2nd Division— the division destined, it will be remembered, to act independently in the Rhodope.

Meanwhile, what was known of the Turks ?

Bulgarian cavalry patrols were unable, of course, to cross the frontier until war had actually been declared; but the summary of information received from deserters, spies and other sources indicated that large hostile bodies were collecting about Adrianople, Kirk Kilisse and in the Ergene valley.

At Adrianople were believed to be concentrating all three *nizam* divisions of the IVth Corps and one or two divisions of *redif*.

At or near Kirk Kilisse appeared to be all three *nizam* divisions of the IIIrd Corps and two or three divisions of *redif*.

And somewhere south of a line drawn between Kirk Kilisse and Adrianople were believed to be at least the four *nizam* divisions of the Ist and IInd Corps and three or four divisions of *redif*; whilst further units were arriving almost daily.

Thus, the total available by the 17th October appeared to be fifteen divisions, or roughly 150,000 men.

About Havsa or Haskeui was reported to be a mass of Turkish cavalry.

This last news was favourable upon the whole. It looked as if the Turks were expecting the main Bulgarian columns to advance down the Tundja, Maritza and Arda valleys, as in the Turkish manœuvre scheme of 1910 ; and as if the possibility of an advance upon Kirk Kilisse more directly from the north was not as yet suspected. Otherwise why should the Turkish cavalry be gathering in such strength near Adrianople and the junction of the valleys ?

Incidentally, these suppositions proved to be not without foundation, for, a few days later, a despatch from the Turkish cavalry commander to his chief was captured; in it the presence of large forces of Bulgarians in the Maritza and Tundja valleys was reported, but no mention was made of Bulgarian troops further east.

* *

*

THE DECLARATION OF WAR.

By the 17th October, then, the concentration of the three Bulgarian armies had been practically completed without molestation.

And on that date the Turks declared war.

Since delay was altogether in their favour, why they should have elected thus to precipitate events is not altogether clear. Had even the frontier troops alone been ready to assume the offensive or had the cavalry intended to raid, there might have been some logic in the measure; but to throw down the gauntlet, as did the Turks, and then fail for four whole days to make a move shows a lack of co-operation between the ministries responsible for foreign politics and war. Political without military initiative is rarely advantageous once hostilities are imminent. Hence the declaration of war should be deferred, as a rule, till the party making it is ready to strike; the two acts should be, if possible, simultaneous, but if not, the declaration should follow rather than precede the blow.

* * * * *

It is interesting to try to trace the reason why the Turks forestalled the Allies in the declaration of war.

During the stage of mobilization European

opinion, as represented in the European Press, was, generally speaking, confident that the Turks in the long run would win. It was allowed that the Allies might score some successes at the outset if they invaded Turkish territory at once; but, when a fortnight passed and nothing happened, the cry began to be raised that the Allies had lost their chance, that the delay had enabled Turkey to establish her *numerical* superiority—and in journalistic circles the value of mere numbers is always overrated; three Dreadnoughts, for instance, must always beat two.

Now the Turkish Press and politicians have little or no expert knowledge of military affairs, but all were clamouring for war. Every Turkish editor, every Turkish politician honestly believed the Turk to be the finest soldier in the world, and the Ottoman army bound to win; and, when opinion abroad began to swing round in their favour, enthusiasm knew no bounds. Eventually, as in July 1870, the agitation became too strong for the Cabinet, political overcame military considerations, and war had to be declared.

Both in 1870 and in 1912 the weaker and less ready side was, then, responsible for beginning the war some days earlier than its interests required. Whether in the long run this fact made much difference to the Turks is, of course, mere speculation. But it shows once again the dangers inherent in the ignorance of Press editors and politicians, and the necessity of ensuring beforehand some discipline amongst them when a national crisis is at hand, and naval or military interests are involved.

* * * * *

Upon receipt of the news of the declaration of war the Bulgarians began to put into execution their long-prepared and carefully thought out plan. Now, although it was hoped that the Turks would be so puzzled by the elaborately complicated measures of concentration of the three Bulgarian armies, that their attention would be drawn rather towards Adrianople than towards Kirk Kilisse, and that consequently their preparations to defend the latter might be found to be behindhand, yet every credit was given to the enemy and every allowance was made for his taking full advantage of the strength of his position.

Whether the attempt to deceive the Turks succeeded or not, the plan remained the same; nothing hinged upon the unknown factor whether the concentration of the Third Army had been successfully concealed or not.

* * * * *

Intelligence services in war can more or less readily ascertain *facts*, that the enemy, for instance, is or is not at certain places; they can ascertain the present or the past, but the future is quite another matter. Actions and facts are one thing, thoughts, and plans, another; for the commander can, and should, keep the latter to himself—a point which, incidentally, is not always borne in mind by those, for instance, who order their patrols to discover and report the enemy's *intentions*.

A sudden and rather unexpected declaration of war by the Turks indicated some offensive action on their part; but what form that action

THE STRATEGICAL DEPLOYMENT 47

would take it was for the moment impossible to foretell. As the Bulgarians did not know the intentions of the Turks it was wisest for them to assume that their adversary would act in the way most inconvenient to themselves, to the execution of their plan. This plan was to mask Adrianople and to take Kirk Kilisse in the first place, and to complete these initial steps in the shortest possible time. The Turks could best obstruct the execution of this plan by great activity around Adrianople and by entrenching and stoutly holding their position at Kirk Kilisse; that is, they were to be expected to operate strategically on the defensive at the outset, using the pivots Adrianople and Kirk Kilisse as breakwaters against the tide of Bulgarian invasion.

In reality they did nothing of the sort; but it was upon these assumptions that General Savoff acted.

* *
*

ADVANCE OF THE SECOND ARMY.

On the 18th October all three Bulgarian armies began to move.

Advanced troops of the Second and First Armies actually crossed the frontier on this day, and the Guard Regiment of cavalry, attached to the former, occupied Mustafa Pasha without opposition the same afternoon. (*See* Map No. 5.)

Now the Maritza above Adrianople is normally about the size of the Thames at Hampton Court; it runs through a low-lying, marshy valley, and during the rainy season is liable to flood. The only bridge across the Maritza between Seimenli in Bulgaria and Adrianople —a distance of nearly 30 miles—is at Mustafa Pasha. Its possession was, consequently, of considerable importance to any force advancing down the valley; especially to a force contemplating siege operations and therefore dragging with it guns too heavy to be put upon pontoons or improvised military bridges. Before retreating the Turkish garrison of Mustafa Pasha attempted to destroy this bridge; but two out of the three charges failed to explode and the third merely chipped a piece off one side of the massive old Roman structure and did no material damage. It is interesting to note that the Turks nearly always failed in their attempts at demolitions; not only were important bridges left intact behind them, but even the telegraph offices and lines were rarely damaged. They appear to have had plenty of explosives but no knowledge how to use them.

* * * * *

With the bridge at Mustafa Pasha captured the Second Army could continue its advance down both sides of the Maritza valley, and carry out its special task, the masking of Adrianople. The Second Army was short of a division at this period— the 11th Division being back at Philippopolis, not yet fully mobilized; consequently the 3rd Division, which was in the Tundja valley north of Adrianople, was for the time being detached from the First to the Second Army.

THE STRATEGICAL DEPLOYMENT 49

Now, as already mentioned, an attack upon Adrianople with the idea of compelling the fortress to surrender formed no part of the intended plan of campaign. Adrianople was to be first masked and then invested—that is, in the first place, the garrison was to be prevented from interfering with the operations or communications of the Bulgarian field armies; and next, it was to be cut off from all outside intercourse and so from its sources of supply.

It was known before the war that the actual fortress troops included some 60 companies of garrison artillery with about 250 heavy guns. It was known also that Adrianople was the headquarters of the Turkish IVth Army Corps, and that this army corps included three divisions of *nizam*, or first line troops, six divisions of *redif*, or second line, two cavalry brigades, and certain corps troops, with a total war strength, on paper, of more than 100,000 fighting men. Definite information, however, was not forthcoming as to how far the mobilization of these units had progressed when war was declared, how many had been concentrated at the corps headquarters, or how many had marched away. Later it became evident that, in addition to the fortress troops, the garrison consisted of approximately three divisions of *nizam* and three of *redif*, with about 300 field and 45 machine guns—a total of, roughly, 60,000 men. But at the moment when the Bulgarians began their advance against the fortress the situation was somewhat vague, and for all they knew the strength of the garrison might have been considerably greater than it eventually proved to be.

* * * * *

FIFTH PROBLEM. My fifth problem, then, is that which faced General Ivanoff, the Commander of the Second Army. How, with a force of three divisions, or, roughly, 90,000 men, to surround a fortress containing a garrison of, perhaps, numerically equal strength? Extend round the circumference of a circle measuring not less than 50 miles, and contain within it a united force, protected by fortifications and enjoying interior lines? Carry out this operation at the least possible risk of defeat in detail, and yet employ the minimum number of men —since every man who could be spared would eventually be required for even more important duties elsewhere?

Ivanoff's solution is worth noting and remembering. He advanced with the utmost caution, taking only one section at a time, and prepared at any moment for a fight. His general plan was to drive the Turks within the girdle of their forts and systematically to close first the western exits, then the northern, then the eastern, and lastly the southern —moving round with the hands of the clock. As each section was occupied the troops allotted to it dug themselves in; when once they were entrenched economies could be effected in their numbers, and thus the line could be gradually lengthened until the circle was complete. During this methodical deployment the troops not yet extended were as far as possible kept in hand to

THE STRATEGICAL DEPLOYMENT 51

form a local reserve; while behind the local reserve was a general reserve in the shape of the First Army, so disposed by the Commander-in-Chief during the opening phases of the campaign as to be able to support either the Second Army or the Third.

* * * * *

Accordingly, after the capture of Mustafa Pasha and its bridge, the 8th Division marched down the right bank of the Maritza, the 9th down the left, whilst the 3rd Division was temporarily held back.

Each of the three divisions was kept as far as possible concentrated, or rather its brigades were so disposed with reference to each other as to be ready at any moment to deploy for a possible encounter, to meet the enemy and at once attack; for a passive defensive on the part of the Turks was not an attitude which could have been with certainty foreseen. Contrary to expectation, however, no serious opposition was encountered, and as the 8th and 9th Divisions approached the fortress they entrenched. As they entrenched and thereby became more secure against counter attack, so the line was gradually extended north. As the 9th Division methodically worked north and then east so the 3rd Division was gradually released to work down south and astride the communications between Adrianople and Kirk Kilisse; but this position was not reached, as will be seen, without a fight.

Until the western, northern and eastern exits from the fortress were closed no serious attempt was made to close the southern; this, the section between the right bank of the Arda and the lower Maritza valley, was merely observed by Taneff's cavalry brigade.

And whilst the western, then northern, then eastern faces of the fortress were being invested by the Second Army, the First Army was kept back about Buyuk Dervent, ready to support it if required.

* * * * *

But the First Army, having lent a division to the Second, was only two divisions strong. Now, the rôle of the Second Army was to mask Adrianople; the rôle of the Third Army was to take Kirk Kilisse; and the First Army was the strategical reserve in the hands of the Commander-in-Chief to be used, according to circumstances, to support either of the other two. This strategical reserve, with its twofold rôle, was looked upon as most important, and the Commander-in-Chief much grudged the loan of a division from it to the Second Army. So much so that he compromised. In order to keep his reserve as strong as possible he determined, whilst lending the 3rd Division to the Second Army, to retain his hold upon one of its brigades. It is interesting to note that he attained this end not by definitely withholding or earmarking a certain brigade, but merely by telling the Second Army Commander that each day *one* of the three brigades of the 3rd Division was to be at his disposal, so that he could call for its services if required. Why this procedure?

The Commander-in-Chief during these initial

THE STRATEGICAL DEPLOYMENT 53

operations remained at Stara Zagora in telegraphic touch with all three armies, marking up all moves upon his map, watching the gradual development of his plan, and modifying it when necessary, but maintaining control only in general terms. With the details of the investment he did not interfere. As the 3rd Division was manœuvring, and gradually working down south, the tasks for its different brigades were varying from day to day, and it was therefore left to the divisional and army commanders to decide which brigade could most conveniently be spared.

* * * * *

Reports appeared in the Press at the time describing heavy fighting during the advance of the Second Army upon Adrianople. In reality there was very little. Two small skirmishes took place with retreating Turkish rear guards, one about Hadikeui on the west, the other near Fikele on the north; but by the 21st October the outlying Turkish troops had all withdrawn behind the girdle of redoubts, and the western and northern faces of the fortress were more or less completely invested.

By this date the First Army, marching slowly, and ready to turn west if required, seems to have reached the vicinity of Tartarlar, the 1st Division leading, the 10th in rear and rather on its right (west). During its comparatively deliberate advance there was some skirmishing near the frontier about Buyuk Dervent but no serious opposition.

* *
*

ADVANCE OF THE THIRD ARMY.

Meanwhile, the Third Army, though starting from a concentration area roughly four times as far from the frontier as that of the First Army, was not brought up immediately into line. Why ?

Because, before attacking Kirk Kilisse, it was deemed sound to make sure that the Adrianople garrison was detained, and that there could be no direct co-operation between it and the Turkish forces further east. Moreover, it was important that the attack upon Kirk Kilisse once begun should be carried straight through to its conclusion without a check, and that therefore every available man should be at hand to support the attack if required.

But the First Army could not support *simultaneously* both armies on its flanks. And until the first step had been completed, until all exits from Adrianople had been sealed by the Second Army, the Commander-in-Chief was not in a position to decide how much or how little from his central manœuvring mass, the First Army, could be spared to support the second step, the storming of Kirk Kilisse by the Third Army.

One thing at a time. The investment of Adrianople was a ticklish business. If the Turks resented being invested it might be necessary to fight, to fight them with the Second Army closely supported by the First. At any rate, until the divisions of the Second Army had made good their objectives, had surrounded Adrianople, and dug themselves in, it was considered unsound to let

THE STRATEGICAL DEPLOYMENT 55

the First Army go far afield, or get involved in other operations.

On the other hand, Kirk Kilisse might prove to be a very hard nut to crack. The Third Army might be sufficient by itself: or it might not. But in any case no risks were to be taken and the first attack upon Kirk Kilisse was to be the main attack, an attack by one army closely supported by another, by two armies in close co-operation, not first by one army and then, if necessary, by another—nothing piecemeal, or disjointed.

Lastly, there were in any case advantages in allowing the more western Bulgarian forces to become engaged earlier than the eastern, the right flank earlier than the left; because, if as was hoped the concentration of the Third Army had been successfully concealed, then the more the Turkish troops about Kirk Kilisse could be induced to face towards the west or north-west, the greater the chance of their exposing their right flank to a sudden descent upon it from the north.

Accordingly the Third Army, like the First, moved slowly at first, and by the 21st October its advanced troops had only reached the vicinity of the frontier, the centre column directed on Kaibilar.

The advance, though comparatively slow, was not an easy one. There were no proper roads and both troops and transport marched more or less straight across country, in an echelon formation, the flank divisions leading, the centre division about a day's march in rear. As the frontier is approached the terrain becomes hilly and very rough and

56 THE CAMPAIGN IN THRACE

broken—so difficult, in fact, that whole companies had sometimes to be turned on to manhandle the vehicles and guns.

* * * * *

The march formations of the Third Army at this period are specially interesting. During the approach to the frontier reports were received of the presence of a large force of Turkish cavalry near Seliolu, from whom possible trouble was anticipated; but, speaking generally, Demitrieff, the Third Army Commander, did not expect to meet with serious opposition north of Kirk Kilisse. However, he marched his army in such a way that he could fight, and fight at once if necessary.

That is to say, his divisions were not strung out in long parallel columns, so that there could be no entry into action until the tails had deployed upon the heads. But the army as a whole, and each division in itself, marched more or less in this formation:—

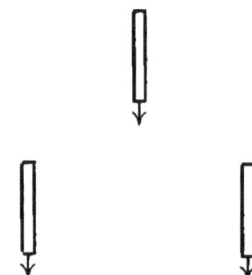

Each column advanced methodically from objective to objective; each was responsible for its own local protection. General security depended not so much on numerous detachments and a strategic

THE STRATEGICAL DEPLOYMENT 57

or general advanced guard, but rather upon *ability to attack*, and to attack quickly and in force, any enemy encountered. Ability, so to speak, to seize the enemy by the throat at once, to protect oneself not by parrying but by thrusting—thrusting, attacking, not with a manœuvring advanced guard whilst the main columns obtain time to deploy, not with a mere detachment liable to be checked and thrown upon the defensive, liable, too, to become involved in such a manner as to dictate a plan of action unsuitable for the main columns in rear, but thrusting, attacking, enveloping with those main columns themselves.

Protection on these principles was advocated in two remarkable lectures given by Colonel de Grandmaison of the French General Staff in February 1911. These lectures were published last year in book form [1] and created a great stir in French and other military circles. Every officer of the Bulgarian General Staff seemed to me to be familiar with this book and to have attempted to put de Grandmaison's theories into practice. So much so that I am inclined to think that some knowledge of these theories is essential to a proper understanding of the conduct of the operations, at any rate of the Bulgarian Third Army. I will return to this point later.

* *
*

[1] "*Deux Conférences*" *faites aux officiers de l'État Major de l'Armée* (Colonel de Grandmaison). Published by Berger-Levrault, Paris, 1912; translated into English by the General Staff, War Office. The author was formerly a professor at the French Staff College, where several prominent Bulgarian officers had been his pupils.

The Cavalry Division.

The Bulgarian cavalry division was last mentioned as holding a protective line from about Kaibilar eastwards towards the sea, with the object of hiding the concentration and line of advance of the Third Army. That mission approached its end as soon as the Third Army was thoroughly on the move, as soon as its leading troops reached the high ground about the frontier and exposed themselves on the skylines, or as soon as its marching columns were liable to detection by the enemy's aerial scouts.

It can rarely be possible, under modern conditions, to conceal for very long the movements of vast armies—this Third Army numbered roughly 80,000. To keep the frontier closed until the columns started from their concentration area, only 30 to 40 miles away, was as much as the cavalry could hope to do. After that the secret was almost bound to come out, even if it was not out already.

And, indeed, there was little necessity for further concealment of the movements of the Third Army, for by the time it reached the frontier it was within two easy marches (easy in point of distance, not more than 25 miles) of its first objective, Kirk Kilisse. Therefore, any big strategical displacements which the Turks might require to make in order to meet this situation must have been already begun if they were to be effective, for large units, army corps and divisions, cannot in practice be moved like pins upon a map; that is to say, the general dispositions, fronts, objectives of whole

THE STRATEGICAL DEPLOYMENT 59

armies cannot undergo very much change in periods of 24 to 48 hours.

Accordingly, the first mission given to the Bulgarian cavalry—the screening of the frontier—began to lose its value; relatively more important missions began to crop up elsewhere. And, therefore, as the Third Army approached the frontier the cavalry division, relieved of this protective rôle, was ordered by the Commander-in-Chief to concentrate upon its right and then to start upon a second mission in the direction of Adrianople.

Exactly what that mission was, I do not know. Perhaps to locate and watch, or engage, that mass of Turkish cavalry reported to be near Seliolu; perhaps to clear up doubts about the situation between Adrianople and Kirk Kilisse; perhaps to help the Second Army in its masking operations. Whatever the mission may have been, it involved concentration and an advance southwest from the frontier about Kaibilar. And this advance, as will be seen, brought it into contact and action with the Turks.

* *
*

FOURTH LECTURE

THE BATTLES OF 22nd-23rd OCTOBER

MAPS.—No. 3, (page 84).

BY the evening of the 21st October the three Bulgarian armies were disposed roughly as under (*see* Map No. 3):—

Second Army.—8th and 9th Divisions approaching the western defences of Adrianople; 11th Division about Philippopolis, its mobilization still incomplete; 3rd Division (attached from the First Army) in the Tundja valley near the frontier, ready to advance south; two of its brigades on the right bank of the Tundja, one on the left.

Directing idea for this army—to surround and mask Adrianople.

Away to the right (west) of the Second Army was a semi-independent detachment consisting of one brigade of the 2nd Division, and advancing from Haskovo on Kirdjali, known to be headquarters of a Turkish *redif* division. (*See* General Map.)

First Army.—1st Division, after some unimportant skirmishing with Turkish cavalry near the frontier during the 19th and 20th October, halted, its left about Sari Talisman; 10th Division in

THE BATTLES OF OCTOBER 22-23

rear and rather to the right (west), its centre near or rather to the north of Buyunli.

Directing idea for this army—to move slowly south, towards Haskeui, ready to support either the Second Army or the Third according to circumstances.

Third Army,—advancing in an echelon formation, its flank divisions forward, its centre division back, thus: 4th Division on the right (west), its centre about Omar Abbas; 5th Division on the left (east), its centre about Terzi Dere; 6th Division in the middle, its centre about Kaibilar.

Directing idea for this army—to advance on and take Kirk Kilisse.

Away to the left (east) of the Third Army was a small independent detachment of frontier troops and volunteers, about 3,000 strong, advancing through the Istrandja Balkan and directed through Geuktepe on Tirnovojik. (*See* Map No. 2.)

Cavalry Division—having completed its first mission, the screening of the Third Army, concentrated, or concentrating, on its own right about Tartarlar, between the right (west) of the Third Army and the left (east) of the First.

* * * * *

During the 18th and 19th October the weather was fine, but on the 20th heavy rain began and continued almost incessantly for the next four days. The bad weather affected the operations in several ways.

The only metalled roads in northern Thrace are the two entering Adrianople from the west, from Mustafa Pasha and from Ortakeui, and those running eastwards from it to Tirnovojik through Kirk Kilisse, and towards Constantinople through Baba Eski; in addition, a metalled road joins Kirk Kilisse with Baba Eski, and another, metalled in places, runs from Kirk Kilisse towards Bunar Hissar, Visa and Sarai. These metalled roads are as rough as can be, but other means of intercommunication are mere tracks which become almost impassable for wheels after heavy rain. From the 20th October onwards, then, all military movements were seriously delayed. The Bulgarians were worse hampered than the Turks, for of all the Bulgarian units only the 9th Division had the advantage of a road. Again, intercommunication, both lateral between neighbouring columns and from front to rear, became extremely difficult. Lastly, reconnaissance became slow and ineffective; for cavalry reconnoitring detachments and patrols lost their bearings in the mist and rain, and either failed to reach distant objectives, or, if they reached them, failed in any case to get their information back in time to be of service. Aeroplanes, had any been available, would have been unable to rise off the seas of mud, or once aloft to have seen what lay below.

Thus the fog of war became thicker than ever; and for information the Bulgarian General Staff had to rely almost entirely on fugitives from Turkish villages and towns, who had left their homes in fear of massacre, and on Christian deserters from the Turkish ranks. Both fugitives and deserters arrived in the Bulgarian camps at all hours of the day, but their reports, based on ignorance and fear, were most conflicting.

By the evening of the 21st October, then, little more was known with any certainty than that great activity prevailed in Adrianople and Kirk Kilisse, and that military movements were in progress between these two places and to their south.

* * *

The Battle of Seliolu.

On the 22nd October the weather in the morning temporarily improved and all three Bulgarian armies continued their advance. Definite contact with the Turks was established this day from Yurush, west of Adrianople, to Erikler, north of Kirk Kilisse, a front of roughly 50 miles; and more or less serious fighting began all along this line.

As in most encounter battles when neither side has time to make, much less to execute, detailed plans, the record of events is most confusing; the following is a mere outline of the main operations.

To take the centre first.

Early in the day the Bulgarian cavalry division, advancing south from about Tartarlar, found and reported large camps of Turkish troops of all arms about Kukiler—that is across the line of advance of the First Army.

The Turks appear to have taken no adequate protective measures and to have been surprised, much in the way that the French were surprised by Rheinbaben's cavalry division west of Metz the day before the battle of Vionville. Roused from their camps, however, the Turks turned out

64 THE CAMPAIGN IN THRACE

and started north, driving back before them the Bulgarian cavalry and gradually becoming engaged with the leading troops of the 1st Division, a few miles north and north-west of Seliolu.

Under cover of this advanced guard fighting the Turks seem to have succeeded in deploying, their right on the hills just east of Seliolu, their left about Gechkenlia. Seliolu itself lies in a valley—practically in a cup. About a brigade appears to have been put upon a knoll just east of the village, but from the extraordinary manner in which the troops of this brigade sited and dug their trenches it is charitable to suppose that they only reached this position in the dark. The remainder of this Turkish force occupied the northern edge of the high ground, partly very open, partly covered with scrub, west and south-west of Seliolu.

The three brigades of the Bulgarian 1st Division seem to have been rather scattered when the action began—on their way, perhaps, each to a different village for shelter for the night—and only two brigades and six batteries took part in the actual battle. The third brigade was drawn into a separate action about Kaipa, to which reference will be made later.

The plan of the Divisional Commander, Tosheff, seems to have been to direct one regiment (four battalions) against what he judged to be the Turkish centre, Seliolu, and with three regiments to envelop the Turkish left. Meanwhile on the Turkish right appeared a brigade of the Bulgarian 4th Division, either attracted by the gun fire or detached from the Third Army to reinforce

THE BATTLES OF OCTOBER 22-23

the First in accordance with instructions from headquarters.

The decisive attack was driven home after nightfall and was completely successful, although the losses were severe. The fighting here formed one of the fiercest incidents in the whole campaign; the 1st (Sofia) Regiment, for instance, which is said by chance to have encountered the 1st (Constantinople) Regiment of the Turks, lost more than 250 in killed alone.

During the night it began again to pour with rain.

By the morning of the 23rd October the Turks in this quarter were in full retreat, south, south-east and south-west, and their retreat rapidly became a rout.

* * * * *

Now the First Army was nominally the strategical reserve in the hands of the Commander-in-Chief—the last of the armies which he wished to see seriously engaged. Partly for this reason, partly, perhaps, owing to exhaustion and bad weather, the First Army halted on the 23rd and made little or no attempt to follow up its victory.

But the cavalry division was admirably placed to take up the pursuit. For when both the First and the Third Armies became engaged on the afternoon of the 22nd, the cavalry was ordered to withdraw from the fighting and to fill the gap between them, and it accordingly concentrated near Keremitlia, a few miles east of Seliolu. Incidentally it is to be noted that both men and horses probably gained thereby a comparatively good night's rest and food.

Advancing the next morning in the pouring rain, they took Yenidje, a large village lying in a hollow with entrenchments on the hills around it; cut down about 600 of those of the retreating Turks who attempted to resist; captured a number of prisoners, about 25 guns and practically the whole of the baggage of the Turkish Ist Corps; and were only checked by fresh troops encountered near Kavakli.

It is probable that this action of the cavalry more than anything else accounted for the panic which spread to Kirk Kilisse and affected all the Turkish troops engaged in these preliminary battles.

* *
*

The Battle of Petra-Erikler.

Meanwhile, another and quite separate engagement was being fought out 8–10 miles east of Seliolu.

The Third Army, as already narrated, advanced in an echelon formation, the 4th and 5th Divisions leading, the former on the right (west) directed on Karamza, the latter on the left (east) directed on Kovchas; the 6th Division between the two and about a day's march in rear.

Near the actual frontier line the ground proved to be exceptionally difficult; so bad, indeed, that only one practicable path could be found for wheels, with the result that the guns and vehicles of the whole army had to converge upon it and be passed through a defile 5 or 6 miles long.

On the afternoon of the 22nd October the leading

THE BATTLES OF OCTOBER 22-23

troops of the 4th and 5th Divisions began to come into touch with the enemy south-east of Karamza and north of Eski Polos and Erikler. No serious fighting took place this day, but by nightfall Erikler had been occupied by the Bulgarians, whilst Eski Polos seems to have remained in the hands of the Turks.

Headquarters of the Bulgarian Third Army, and of the 4th Division spent the night at Karamza. One brigade of this division went off, as mentioned above, to take part in the neighbouring battle of Seliolu.

Eski Polos is a fair-sized village, lying at the foot of a comparatively isolated sugar-loaf hill or peak, and this peak, crowned by the ruins of an ancient fortress, is an outstanding feature in the landscape. It commands a view over the surrounding country for many miles and can itself be seen from the Lule Burgas battlefield, for instance, nearly 40 miles further south, and from the heights round Adrianople. If only as an observation point its possession was of considerable tactical importance.

During the night the Turks entrenched, in a very perfunctory fashion, along a ridge, or series of ridges extending, not without gaps, from Kadikeui to just south of Eski Polos, and thence to a point a mile or two west of Petra; the heavy rain, however, must have filled the trenches with water as fast as they were dug.

On the morning of the 23rd October the Bulgarians renewed their attack. Eski Polos hill and village were soon captured and the general

68 THE CAMPAIGN IN THRACE

plan then became to pivot on Eski Polos and gradually to develop a decisive attack upon the Turkish left. It seems that only on this flank, on a ridge just south-west of Petra, did the Turks make any serious resistance. Elsewhere the collapse was rapid and by the evening had developed into a disorderly retreat upon Kirk Kilisse, if not exactly a rout. The Turkish artillery, which appears to have kept far back on the Petra ridge and to have made little attempt to support its infantry, went off early in the battle and so escaped capture for one day; but most of the transport of what turned out to be the Turkish Third Army Corps was taken in Petra village.

On the other flank also, east of the Teke Dere, the Turks were driven back, less quickly, perhaps, for the ground was rough and rocky, and ideal for rear guard fighting.

The leading Bulgarian troops pushed forward in the evening to within two or three miles of Kirk Kilisse, but the general order was to halt at nightfall and re-organize in expectation of serious fighting on the morrow — the attack, in fact, upon the much talked of forts and position of Kirk Kilisse. This order failed to reach one company till, in the dark, it had arrived almost at the outskirts of the town; but on receipt of the order it withdrew.

Headquarters of the Third Army spent the night of the 23rd in Petra, General Demitrieff sleeping in the room where Mahmud Mukhtur Pasha had slept the night before. The General Staff of the Third Army appears to have been unaware this night of the important success already gained by the First Army away to their right.

* * * * *

The Capture of Kirk Kilisse.

The following morning, the morning of the 24th October, Kirk Kilisse was occupied without further opposition, for during the night the Turks had all stampeded.

Why, remains more or less a mystery. There are several theories. One, for instance, is to the effect that the appearance of the Bulgarian company on the outskirts of the town the evening before had started the rumour of a night attack, and that this rumour caused the panic. Another version is that consternation was spread by the arrival of refugees from Seliolu with news of the disaster there, of the vigorous pursuit by the Bulgarian cavalry, and of its capture of Yenidje, whereby the line of retreat was threatened. Greek inhabitants of the town informed me that amongst the Turks the cry was often raised in the streets that night, " Look out; be quick; the cavalry are coming!"

Kirk Kilisse was duly occupied by the Bulgarian 6th Division. The 4th and 5th Divisions, passing respectively west and east of the town, became engaged about midday with Turkish rearguards on the line Kavakli–Uskubdere, but there was no serious resistance. And on this line the Bulgarian Third Army eventually halted for three days.

* *
*

BATTLES OF KAIPA AND YURUSH.

Meanwhile, away in the west an effort had been made by the Adrianople garrison to co-operate with the Turkish operations elsewhere.

A force estimated at two, or even three, whole Turkish divisions (a Turkish division is about the equivalent of a Bulgarian brigade) marched out from cover of the forts on the 22nd October and advanced north-east towards Kaipa. Here they were met by two Bulgarian brigades—one of the 3rd Division, one of the 1st—and after some serious fighting were driven back upon the defences. The Turks are said to have suffered very heavily in this engagement, one column being caught by surprise artillery fire and almost decimated.

About the same time a force of some six battalions attacked portions of the Bulgarian 8th Division west of Adrianople near Yurush, but were repulsed without much difficulty.

* * * * *

Thus the fighting between the 22nd and 24th October ended in the repulse of the sorties from Adrianople and another step forward in the investment of the fortress; in the capture of Kirk Kilisse, of about 50 guns of various patterns, of vast stores of small arms, ammunition, equipment and provisions, two aeroplanes, and close upon 2,000 prisoners; and in the utter demoralization of what were presumed to be the Turkish advanced troops, covering the concentration of the main masses in their rear.

* *
*

THE SITUATION AT HEADQUARTERS.

Now go back to General Headquarters, still at Stara Zagora—more than 60 miles from Adrianople, more than 90 from Kirk Kilisse. And remember the general plan—to mask Adrianople, to take Kirk Kilisse and then meet the main Turkish mass, wherever that might be; remember also the rôles allotted to the three armies.

Imagine, then, the tenor of the reports received by General Savoff and his staff during these four days, 21st–24th October. Neither frequent, nor detailed reports, for these—so they informed me—were neither called for nor required. Each army was expected to send twice, or at most three times, in twenty-four hours a general summary of its situation, and no more.

At first, the weather fine, intercommunication easy and all going well. Mustafa Pasha captured with unexpected ease, and the Second Army making more rapid progress than the circumstances justified; the First Army meeting with some minor opposition on the frontier—nothing to excite much comment and easily brushed away.

Then on the 20th and 21st October the heavy rain; roads, or rather tracks, becoming quagmires; march tables becoming problematical; intercommunication slower and less sure; reconnaissance disappointing—the fog of war getting thicker, not thinner, as the troops advance.

Next, on the evening of the 22nd, reports of serious fighting around Adrianople—the Turks beginning to strike back. The 3rd Division, its units divided by the Tundja River, unbridged and unfordable, and the water rising every hour; an attack developing upon those troops who were already on the eastern bank, and were therefore somewhat dangerously exposed. Will it be necessary to support them? To reinforce the Second Army with troops from the general reserve, the First?

But a little later reports arrive that the First Army, too, is engaged—seriously engaged; by midnight of the 22nd–23rd its casualties must have reached at least a thousand.

A little later still come reports from the Third Army that it, too, is becoming engaged about Erikler and Eski Polos—earlier than was either expected or intended. General Demitrieff is known to be of a somewhat impetuous disposition. Is he, perhaps, getting a little out of hand? The attack upon Kirk Kilisse, remember, was expected to be a very serious undertaking; not to be commenced until the " all's clear " signal came from the Second Army, around Adrianople, and so released the First Army and enabled it to be ready to support the Third.

* * * * *

In less than 48 hours, then, the whole situation has more or less completely changed. Nothing shaping out quite as had seemed most probable; all a little perplexing; events moving at an unexpectedly rapid pace, and in the wrong chronological order.

Comparing the strategical plan for the invasion of Thrace as a whole with a tactical plan of attack,

THE BATTLES OF OCTOBER 22–23

we see the general reserve getting engaged as soon as, or even sooner than, the firing lines; the decisive attack upon the enemy's right flank developing prematurely.

* * * * *

Such, then, roughly, was the situation as it appeared to General Headquarters on the 23rd October. Does it call for any fresh instructions, any change of plan?

General Savoff decided to let things take their course. The scheme was essentially simple and straightforward, sufficiently elastic to cover a multitude of unforeseen events, and General Savoff determined to adhere to it.

Interference with the way in which events were shaping themselves seemed to be required at one point alone. The First Army was the reserve army, and the reserve army for the present it must remain. Therefore, in spite of the news which must have reached headquarters by the morning of the 23rd October of the repulse of the sorties from Adrianople and of the striking success at Seliolu, the First Army is ordered to halt, to re-organize, to resume its position in reserve.

* * * * *

Later must have come reports of the victories of the Third Army at Eski Polos, Erikler and Petra; of the Turks in this quarter also being in retreat; of their outlying troops being driven back upon the entrenchments of Kirk Kilisse.

Finally arrives on the morning of the 24th October the most dramatic and unexpected news of all—the capture of Kirk Kilisse.

74 THE CAMPAIGN IN THRACE

About the same time, too, must have been received the news of the great Servian victory at Kumanovo.

What instructions should General Savoff issue now? That is the sixth big problem I put before you.

SIXTH PROBLEM.

* * * * *

Briefly, there seem to have been two main alternatives.

To push on at once, pursue; the Turks were obviously demoralized and on the run—to keep them on the run.

Or, to halt, reorganize and concentrate before moving further south; having completed the first two steps of the plan, the masking of Adrianople and the capture of Kirk Kilisse, to get the armies together and in hand before advancing to the third and most important step, the battle with the main Turkish mass.

It must have been clear by this time that the Turks, encountered and defeated at various points along the frontier during the last four days, included all or portions of the Ist, IInd, IIIrd and IVth Army Corps, the four corps belonging to Thrace. It was a reasonable, and certainly the safest, assumption to make that these were the covering troops; and that behind them would be concentrating numerous other corps. If these covering troops were really hopelessly beaten and demoralized, and if they could be, and were, closely followed, then their demoralization might well infect the troops in rear; the rout might even continue right away to Constantinople; a stand, if made at all, would be made by men already half defeated.

A pursuit might complete the Turkish collapse and prevent a rally. That was looking at things in their most favourable light.

On the other hand the bulk of the Third Army, near Kirk Kilisse, was by this time 20–25 miles from the bulk of the First Army, about and west of Seliolu—and this distance in bad weather and without roads is, for a large force, a two days' march.

The First Army, too, was still short of a division lent to the Second Army.

The investment of Adrianople was incomplete, for its southern and south-eastern sides were still open.

Behind the retreating Turkish troops might be found the enemy's main mass, entrenched and staunch. If so, the Third Army would come into action against it unsupported, and would risk defeat in detail; or, at any rate, the two Bulgarian armies would begin the battle piecemeal, both more or less exhausted, in more or less disorder, and probably short of supplies—not the best way in which to begin a big battle and to win.

Lastly, the retreating Turks had taken not one direction but many, south, south-east and south-west. Which of these directions would bring the Bulgarians up against their next objective, the Turkish mass, was at present far from certain; and the selection of a wrong direction might lead to disadvantageous if not disastrous results.

General Savoff decided to adhere to his original plan; to play what seemed to be the safer and more certain game; to locate the Turkish mass before attempting to strike it; and, when striking, to strike with his full force, suitably disposed, re-organized, well supplied and rested.

General Demitrieff was ready and anxious to push on at once, for the capture of Kirk Kilisse had solved his problems of supply. But the Commander-in-Chief put his foot down and ordered the Third Army, like the First Army, to halt; whilst the cavalry division was sent off on a mission of exploration, was sent off to find the main Turkish mass.

* * * * *

That was a most momentous decision, affecting the whole course of the war.

For we know now that at this period *there was no Turkish mass*; that the Bulgarian cavalry were sent to search for what was a mere bogey, when they started. To all intents and purposes the Turks defeated on the 22nd–23rd October were not covering troops, but the main Turkish army, such as it was; and there were practically no formed or formidable bodies in their rear. The collapse of the Turks, for the time being at any rate, was complete; they were retreating in the utmost confusion and disorder.

Had the Bulgarian Third Army been ordered to advance at once towards Constantinople, and had the First Army closely followed; had they been *able* to do so—to advance and keep on advancing, largely a question of supplies—it seems possible that the campaign in Thrace might have been finished in a fortnight.

The four days' halt after the capture of Kirk Kilisse enabled the Turks more or less to pull themselves together, to organize further serious resistance along the line of the Karagach stream. This resistance eventually checked the Bulgarians for nearly ten days, including the second halt which became necessary after the big battle had been fought. Add these ten days to the other four and the total time lost was at least a fortnight. A fortnight was just sufficient for the lines of Tchatalja to be properly fortified and manned—and only these lines prolonged the war.

In other words, without the four days' respite after their defeats upon the frontier the Turks would probably not have stood behind the Karagach; and had they failed to stand behind the Karagach they might never have succeeded in holding the Tchatalja lines.

All this of course is speculation; but speculation based on reasonable probabilities and on wisdom after the events.

* * * * *

General Savoff, then, failed to appreciate the situation rightly. Not *knowing* the facts of the case he had to guess—and guessed wrong.

It is easy to criticize this decision.

But given the strategical situation in Thrace when hostilities began, the advantages on the side of the Turks, their military reputation as it stood before the war, who would have guessed that their whole scheme of defence had been shattered in three days?

General Demitrieff was ready and anxious to push

on, and General Savoff stopped him. It seems now that the former was right and the latter wrong, so that when history comes to be written it is not unlikely that General Savoff will be severely criticized and blamed.

But we must think twice before learning any lessons from the record of these events. It would be rash to deduce any principles or rules; to affirm in this instance that the enemy being on the run must be kept on the run; and that, therefore, General Demitrieff in principle was right and General Savoff wrong.

Both generals thought that the defeated troops were covering troops, that is a detachment; and, if detachments chase detachments, it becomes difficult to arrange co-operation as a whole. General Savoff aimed at combining the action of two or three units (armies), at making them strike a blow *together*; and to do so he was compelled to restrain the movements of the leading unit.

The fog of war at the time was very thick. The Commander-in-Chief had to guess and guessed wrong. Luck was against him, and we all know what luck means in sport and war.

*   *   *   *   *

Could the fog have been kept any thinner, or more rapidly dispelled?

Cavalry patrols, pushed out during the battles around and beyond the enemy's flanks, might have cleared up the situation in his rear; might have discovered that what were believed to be covering troops were actually covering nothing.

THE BATTLES OF OCTOBER 22–23

But small patrols have little penetrative power; they are easily blocked, both going and returning. Hence small patrols must have been numerous to enable at least a percentage to succeed.

The alternative is to employ a large detachment, to depend upon force not guile.

Either alternative, a large number of small patrols or a large detachment, means a corresponding reduction in the strength of the available cavalry, and, all told, the Bulgarians had only three brigades—including the divisional cavalry a proportion of about 5,000 sabres to 230,000 rifles. Had they reduced the strength of the cavalry division, for instance, during or prior to the battle of Seliolu, the weaker would have been the force which eventually pursued—the less decisive would have been the battle. You cannot have your cake and eat it.

Cavalry reconnaissance is a slow process at its best; slower in war than in peace. It takes time for the patrols to reach their objectives, to discover what they can; time to get their information back; time to piece together the various items at headquarters, and draw deductions from the whole. On the morning of the 24th October *early* information was essential; if the Third Army was to follow the defeated Turks, the sooner the orders were issued for the start the better; touch once lost might never be regained.

Here, then, was the opportunity for air craft. On the bare, open, rolling downs of Thrace nothing in good weather could remain hidden from an observer in the air.

One or two successful flights by aeroplanes would have laid bare the whole situation; would have fully exposed the deplorable condition of the Turks; would have relieved General Savoff of any necessity to guess—and might therefore have changed the whole course of the campaign.

* * * * *

The Bulgarians, however, had no aeroplanes. Two Turkish aeroplanes were captured in apparently good order at Kirk Kilisse, but no pilot could be found.

With a population of 4,000,000 and a revenue of £5,000,000 the Bulgarians had managed to maintain a peace establishment of 60,000 men and to build up a war establishment of over 400,000 fully trained men. Those are remarkable figures, unequalled elsewhere. Compare them with our own, taking the United Kingdom only, not the Empire. Our population is eleven times, our revenue thirty times, as great as those of Bulgaria; excluding the territorial army, we can put in the field an expeditionary force about one third the size of the Bulgarian field army; and the annual upkeep of the organization necessary to provide this force costs us about thirteen times as much as her normal military budget costs Bulgaria.

The strictest economy was obviously essential. Aeroplanes the Bulgarians could not afford—they were waiting for the prices to come down. Cavalry, too, is an expensive arm; the number had to be kept proportionally low.

Neither flying corps nor cavalry brigades can be

created after hostilities begin, for the very nature of their duties demands long and careful training.

When war became inevitable the Bulgarians bought up aeroplanes from any one prepared to sell. They attempted to extemporize at least the nucleus of a flying corps. It was very expensive, very inefficient; and it only arrived upon the scenes after the decisive phase was ended.

There is no new lesson in all this. For war you can *rely* only upon what you are prepared to maintain in peace—and no more.

* * *

The Turkish Movements.

To turn for a moment to the Turks.

The strategical deployment of the Bulgarian armies was based largely upon the assumption that the Turks would do what in the circumstances seemed to be the best they could do, namely, as already stated, to act strategically on the defensive at first, hold Adrianople and Kirk Kilisse strongly, and use these pivots as breakwaters against the tide of invasion.

The Bulgarians' plan of coping with the situation as they expected to find it, was so simple and logical, and so consistently and methodically carried out that it seems probable that their combinations would have succeeded, in all circumstances; still, no doubt their losses at Kirk Kilisse, had this place been defended, would have been heavy, and they might have been considerably delayed.

Actually, the Turks did nothing of the sort.

Instead of taking advantage of the frontier defences, and of compelling the Bulgarians to knock their heads against the forts and field works whilst the Turkish measures of mobilization and concentration were completed further south, Abdulla Pasha, commanding the Thracian army, seems suddenly to have ordered the advance of all who were ready.

Consequently, on the 21st October the Turks moved forward in apparently two main columns, the IIIrd Corps under Mahmud Mukhtar Pasha from Kirk Kilisse towards Petra and Erikler, the Ist from Yenidje towards Tartarlar. The IVth Corps seems to have remained about Havsa, south-west of, and nominally ready to support, the Ist Corps; the IInd Corps about Kavakli, nominally ready to support the IIIrd.

Exactly what Abdulla Pasha's plan was heaven only knows. It is certainly difficult to trace any plan in the record of the Turkish moves or in the Thracian army's operation orders, which were captured a few days later at Kirk Kilisse. But the underlying notions seem to have been first, at all costs to take the offensive and second, to envelop. According to Major von Hochwaechter, an officer of Mahmud Mukhtar Pasha's staff, who was in Kirk Kilisse on the 21st October and there met Abdulla Pasha, the lines of advance of the various Bulgarian columns had by that time been located with more or less accuracy.

At the back of the Turkish mind, then, seems to have been the idea that it was essential to attack; and that, if in doing so the net was spread sufficiently wide, the enemy might be caught within it and destroyed. Now Abdulla Pasha was a protégé of Field Marshal von der Goltz, and had himself spent several years in Prussia; so, too, had Mahmud Mukhtar Pasha and many other influential Turkish officers, commanding units or upon the staff. In the German field service regulations, translated into Turkish almost word for word, great stress is laid throughout on the value of the offensive and the advantages of the enveloping attack. These Turkish officers clearly had some inkling of the spirit of their regulations, but no knowledge or experience of their application to concrete cases in the field.

It is no doubt in principle sound to attack and on principle sound to envelop—if you can; but there are also other principles of the art of war, all of which must receive due consideration, and all must be applied with strong, practical common sense.

A blind adherence to the spirit of ill-digested theories and regulations seems, more than anything else, to have contributed to the series of disasters which befell the Turks during the first week of this campaign.

* * * * *

One other point in passing.

Because the Turkish army was trained nominally on German lines, and because the Turkish army failed, there is a tendency in some quarters to discredit so-called German principles and doctrine; a tendency to go even further and affirm that because the Turkish army proved inefficient, consequently the German army too must be inefficient, or at any rate less efficient than has hitherto been supposed.

There is danger and no logic in reasoning of this nature.

The principles of strategy and tactics are really the same in all armies. We all study the same wars, we all read each other's books, and we all arrive at more or less the same conclusions. The efficiency of an army must be judged, then, not by its regulations but by its ability to put them into practice—and nothing that has happened in the Balkans can throw any light upon the ability of the German army to do that.

* *
*

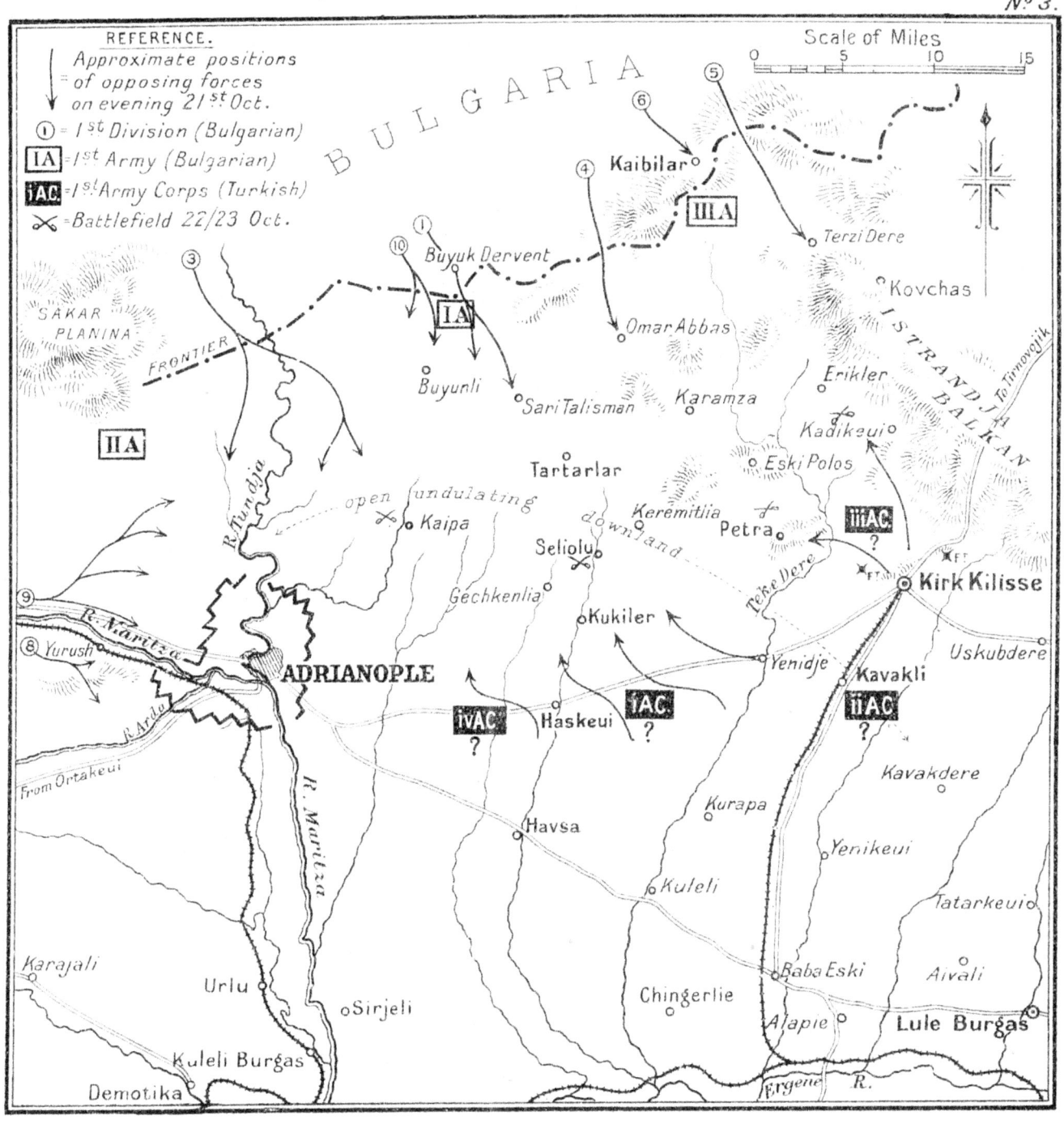

FIFTH LECTURE

THE BATTLE OF LULE BURGAS—BUNAR HISSAR

MAPS.—No. 2, (page 98). No. 4, (page 138).

THE evening of the 24th October found the Bulgarian forces disposed roughly as follows:—

Second Army.—8th and 9th Divisions investing the southern, western, and northern faces of Adrianople; 11th Division still at Philippopolis; 3rd Division (attached) beginning to close the eastern exits after repulsing the sortie of the garrison in the neighbourhood of Kaipa.

First Army.—1st and 10th Divisions halted in the neighbourhood of Seliolu, where two days previously the former had fought and defeated the Turkish 1st Corps.

Third Army.—halted in the area Kirk Kilisse-Kavakli–Uskubdere; 5th Division on the left (east); 6th Division in the centre, but later being transferred to the right (west); 4th Division at first on the right and eventually in the centre.

In these positions the armies remained, more or less at rest, during the next three days; whilst General Headquarters, taking advantage of the lull in the proceedings, moved forward from Stara Zagora to Kizil Agatch.

The situation has many parallels in history and may be compared, for instance, to that of the German armies after the fighting of the 18th August, 1870. Where was now the enemy's main mass? Preparing to cover its capital directly? Or preparing to take up a flank position either behind the Ergene river, based upon Rodosto; or, perhaps, along the foothills of the Istranja Balkan, based upon Midia? Or else where? The cavalry must go and see.

* * * * *

THE CAVALRY RECONNAISSANCE.

Accordingly, Taneff's cavalry brigade was sent off to scour the country south of Adrianople, and in course of time reported Demotika, Dedeagatch and Usun Kopru clear of all but small detachments.

Nazlumoff's division, checked after its pursuit on the 23rd October about Kavakli, had spent the 24th October in harassing the Turks retreating from Kirk Kilisse, and had reached that night the vicinity of Yenikeui, 15 miles south-south-west of Kirk Kilisse.

Thence it advanced south and, after some further skirmishing with parties of retreating Turks, on the morning of the 25th October entered Baba Eski and a little later Mandra junction, capturing in this area 4 engines and about 200 trucks—rolling stock which became invaluable to the Bulgarian supply services during subsequent operations. At a point just east of Mandra the main line was temporarily destroyed in order definitely to sever railway communication between Constantinople and the Adrianople garrison. Meanwhile from this centre, Mandra, the cavalry division pushed out detachments directed upon three main strategical points, viz:—

Malgara through Airobol,
Rodosto, and
Tchorlu, along the railway.

These detachments were given no vague instructions, " to clear up the situation," or " to reconnoitre towards the sea," or " to discover the enemy's intentions "; but a series of clear and precise questions, calling for equally clear and precise replies, " is or is not, the enemy in force in the vicinity of these important road and railway junctions " ?

From Mandra the cavalry division itself moved forward slowly towards Rodosto. An encounter with the bulk of the Turkish cavalry, which had taken little or no part in the battles of the 22nd–23rd October, was fully expected, but, to the surprise of the Bulgarians, no signs of it were seen.

* * * * *

Meanwhile, the general scheme for strategical reconnaissance was completed by the action of the Third Army in sending detachments from Kirk Kilisse towards Bunar Hissar and Visa. But as this army was very short of mounted troops—only one weak squadron of cavalry and one company of mounted gendarmes to each division—the radius of its activity was necessarily somewhat restricted. The limitations are well illustrated by an incident which occurred upon the 25th October, when a small patrol reported that down in a ravine just west of Yeno was a whole battery of quick-firing guns, deserted by its personnel but lying within range of the Turkish outposts. Having no cavalry left in hand, General Demitrieff sent out a force of mounted gunners who succeeded in bringing back, from under the noses of the Turks, five out of six of the deserted guns.

* * * * *

The results of the reconnaissances carried out during the 24th–26th October were:—

negative information from the directions Demotika-Usun Kopru-Airobol;

positive information from the directions Lule Burgas-Visa.

Positive information does not mean clear, complete information, the sort of information which commanders always hope to get and never do in war—so many Turks of this or that division or corps, holding such and such places, in such and such strength. On the contrary the difference between positive and negative information rarely amounts to more than that, whereas in certain directions the cavalry detachments have been able to make ground, in others they have not.

Airmen from aloft or secret agents from within may be able to furnish fuller details, but cavalry patrols can do little more than feel the fringe, find the enemy's outpost line, define the " contour," as the French say. To pierce this contour by land— by air is another matter—and then see what lies beyond it must usually involve fighting; and to fight successfully requires force, the whole cavalry division, for instance, not detached squadrons, troops, patrols. But only information which is vital and which cannot be obtained in any other way should as a rule be *fought* for by detached or independent cavalry, that is, by cavalry acting alone; because the object of all units, all arms, all bodies of armed men is to fight *in close co-operation*, not independently, in detachments, one by one. " The full power of an army can be exerted only when all its parts act in close combination," say our field service regulations early in the book, but they fail, perhaps, to lay sufficient stress upon this principle when, later, they deal with the duties of cavalry in war. Hence there seems to be a tendency in our army to think that, because modern cavalry are fully equipped with firearms and are capable nowadays of conducting and winning minor engagements by themselves, that therefore they can fight independently with *less* disadvantages than they could before.

That notion is a dangerous one. For wars are won and lost by the big battle, not by adding up the sum of the secondary successes; only goals count in war, tries and subsidiaries go for nothing.

By all means let cavalry fight battles by themselves, independently, when the circumstances demand independent action—but be certain that they really do demand it. Independent actions, independent successes all cost men, horses, energy —all to be deducted from fighting power as a whole, from prospects of decisive success, when the big battle eventually takes place. Be certain that the game is worth the candle.

* * * * *

By the 26th October, then, the Bulgarian cavalry were able to define roughly the enemy's contour. Information as to what was taking place behind that contour they did not get. By fighting they might have pierced the contour, and, having pierced it, they might have discovered the dispositions of the main Turkish columns in its rear; they might or might not—in neither case, in neither the piercing of the contour nor in the discovery of the main columns, was success assured.

Was this information, the location of the main Turkish columns, of vital importance at this particular moment—i.e. before the advance began again—to the Bulgarian General Headquarters?

I think not.

To fight, for instance, and thereby discover and report that on the 26th October the Turkish IVth Corps was at Lule Burgas and the Turkish IIIrd Corps near Visa would be to provide important, but not vital, information. Such information might be useful, yet it might, on the other hand, be useless or even worse than useless, because corps which were at Visa and Lule Burgas on the 26th October would not necessarily be at either of these places on the 28th. And yet, as the opposing armies were roughly two days' march apart, the 28th was likely to be about the earliest day upon which a battle could begin. Information as to the enemy's dispositions *during or immediately before* the battle may be vital; it can seldom matter to the same degree, to a vital degree, what they were two days or more before the forces come into contact.

BATTLE OF LULE BURGAS

I labour this point because the craze for information can so easily be overdone.

It is always the commander least decided in his own mind who requires the most information; and whose mental equilibrium is most easily upset when, as so often is the case, he fails to get it.

"Timely information regarding the enemy's dispositions is an essential factor of success in war," say our field service regulations; and in another place, " decisive success in battle can be gained only by a vigorous offensive." It must be recognized, however, that these two conceptions are to a certain extent conflicting. In order to develop an offensive frame of mind it is essential to cultivate the habit of deciding upon definite action *without knowing the enemy's dispositions ;* and of carrying through that action to its logical conclusion, *in spite of* the enemy, however much the enemy by his moves or dispositions attempts to interfere. To await " timely information regarding the enemy's dispositions " may often mean nothing more than to wait to be attacked, to lose the initiative at the outset. This, obviously, must be the result of waiting when operating against an enemy himself imbued with a truly offensive spirit.

* * * * *

Nazlumoff's cavalry division did not attempt unsupported to break through the Turkish outpost lines; and General Savoff appears to have been satisfied to hear from the cavalry the external contour of the Turkish dispositions—not their details.

The reports received from the cavalry when

added to information received from other sources, began to make it clear by the evening of the 26th October that the bulk of the hostile forces were on, or somewhere east of, the general line Lule Burgas–Bunar Hissar; and that no bodies of importance remained in the area between this line and the forts of Adrianople.

* * * * *

Information about the enemy was, presumably, not the only information sought for at this period. Topographical reports were probably also required.

South and east of Kirk Kilisse the country opens out into undulating downland, with all the drainage from north to south into the Ergene river; and the valleys, through which run the little streams, are generally wide and open. Most of the low-lying land has at some time or other been under cultivation, and therefore cleared of scrub; and here cover from fire and view is limited to the folds of the ground. Where on the tops of the ridges the turf remains untouched the scrub is fairly thick in places, but nowhere so thick as to be an obstacle to movement. North of the Kirk Kilisse–Visa road the slopes of the Istranja Balkan begin, and the hills become stony, rough, and practically impassable for wheels. South of the Adrianople–Lule Burgas–Tchorlu road is the Ergene river, lying for the greater part of its course between steep banks and unfordable, at any rate, after rain. The flanks of the Turks appeared, then, to rest upon two obstacles—the Istranja Balkan on the north, the Ergene on the south.

The two roads mentioned above are the only

BATTLE OF LULE BURGAS

roads. The northern one was under construction when the war began, and its roadway had been completed for not more than 10 miles from Kirk Kilisse, to a point a little short of Yeno. Along the southern one, a motor car could just keep going in good weather.

* * * * *

Seventh Problem. The above, then, were, briefly, the dispositions of the Bulgarian armies on the 26th October; the information available of the enemy; and the knowledge of the ground. Intention—to attack, to fight a decisive battle, to complete the scheme of invasion. Required a plan.

That is my seventh problem. How advance and how attack?

* * * * *

The Plan of Attack

The Bulgarian armies being well in hand and well disposed with reference to each other, one plan seems almost to suggest itself. Frontal attack by the Third Army; envelopment of the Turkish left (south) by the First; and as many troops as possible withdrawn from the Second Army in order to support the First, and to form, or add to, the general reserve.

An alternative plan consisted in a frontal attack by the First Army and in an attempt to envelop the Turkish right (north) with the Third Army.

But the Turkish left flank was weaker, and more in the air than was its right. The enemy's main lines of communication lay behind their flanks, but those behind the left flank—the railway and the roads to Rodosto and Tchorlu—were of more importance and at the same time more exposed than those behind their right. Further, and this, perhaps, was the deciding factor, Adrianople had to be borne in mind. Although the fortress was by this time more or less invested, the line round it was very weak, especially on the eastern side. The distance from Adrianople to Lule Burgas is little more than 40 miles, or two long marches by the available road ; and there was, therefore, every possibility of an attempt by the fortress garrison to co-operate with the Turkish forces in the field. The greater the weight with which the Bulgarians pressed against the Turkish right the more would the two hostile masses, the field army and the garrison, tend to come together ; the greater the weight against their left the more they would tend to drift asunder. Now the farther two forces attempting to co-operate can be kept apart, and the greater the intervening mass, the less, as a rule, their effective co-operation.

* * * * *

Of these two obvious alternatives—there may be others—General Savoff selected the first.

His plan, then, was to engage the Turks along their front with the three divisions of the Third Army. These were to advance against the hostile outpost line or contour, drive it back, definitely locate the main bodies sheltering behind it, and by attacking to pin them to their ground. Then, when the Turks were at grips and fully committed along their front, the two available divisions of

BATTLE OF LULE BURGAS

the First Army were to strike in upon the enemy's left or southern flank, and drive him entirely off his main lines of communication towards the Istranja Balkan and the Black Sea Coast. Meanwhile, the Second Army would encircle Adrianople and keep back the garrison within the girdle of its forts.

That briefly was the Bulgarian general plan, to be borne in mind throughout the five days' heavy fighting which ensued. It was nothing if not simple, and was consistently and logically carried out. That it failed in its final purpose the Turks have largely to thank not themselves but the weather.

* * * * *

Measures to Mislead the Turks

As before (*see page* 33), having selected one of two fairly obvious plans, there were many advantages in inducing the enemy to expect the selection of the other.

How was this to be done?

The foreign correspondents accompanying an army in the field are sometimes, though very rarely, a blessing in disguise. Now was the time to use them. The representative of a certain journal, prepared, in his anxiety to get sensational news, to swallow any lie, was made the principal agent.

The small detachment of frontier troops and volunteers advancing through Tirnovojik on Samakov was magnified into an army; and the press of all Europe was soon blazoning forth the news that the Bulgarian main advance was pushing on to Midia and Visa, and that the right of the Turks was being turned.

Later, as will be seen, a further step was taken towards deceiving the Turks as to the flank upon which the decisive stroke would fall.

* *
*

System of Command

The system of command should be noted. General Headquarters still remained at Kizil Agatch, some fifty miles in rear of the manœuvring armies.

Fifty miles—the distance from London to Brighton, or to Cambridge; and imagine what that distance meant before the days of railway trains or motor cars, or even coaches. Here, at Kizil Agatch, telegraphic reports were received from all directions, from all three armies and detachments, and here the Commander-in-Chief decided on the general plan.

The general plan was then issued, confidentially, to army commanders, and with it orders for the

BATTLE OF LULE BURGAS

armies to reach certain areas by certain times. On reaching these areas, the three armies would be so disposed with reference to each other, to the ground and to the position, or supposed position, of the Turks as to be able to carry out the general plan.

With the details of the *execution* of the plan the Commander-in-Chief did not interfere; they were left to the army commanders, to the initiative of the men upon the spot. The Commander-in-Chief supplied, so to speak, only the information and the intention, or plan, paragraphs of the general operation order for the battle; and left the remaining paragraphs blank.

Some of us realize the difficulty of drafting the second, or intention, paragraph of a normal operation order; others do not, and are inclined to slur it over. But get that paragraph clear, precise, apposite, based upon a sound judgment of the situation, then the rest is often easy; the subordinate commanders, the troops themselves will do the rest—all working well and together if they know exactly for what they are working, what the general intention or plan really is.

* * * * *

Incidentally, *plan* seems to me to be a far better word than *intention* here. A plan is a resolution. The word savours more of military precision and determination, and leaves fewer loopholes for a commander to remain vague and undecided in his own mind. Intentions are often laudable, most men mean well; but good intentions are not nearly as helpful to all concerned in military operations as good plans. Nor are the latter as easily and lightly made. To say, for instance, that "the intention is to defeat the enemy" is to say nothing very enlightening, nor calling for much thought; it is neither mischievous nor useful; but to say that "the plan is to defeat the enemy" is an obviously absurd and incomplete remark to make.

The plan, of course, is not necessarily published at all in the operation order; it may be essential to keep the plan or portions of it secret, or to make it known to those concerned by some other means than a formal operation order. But published or kept secret, written down or merely borne in mind, the commander should always have some definite action in view; and that action is better formulated in the shape of a plan than a mere intention.

* * * * *

General Savoff, then, took upon his own shoulders the responsibility of deciding the general plan. Its execution was left to the army commanders, each commanding his own army during the approach march, but the senior (General Demitrieff) assuming command of both armies and of the cavalry division as soon as contact with the Turks was gained, as soon as strategy ended and tactics began.

The battles of October 22nd–23rd had been fought by the two armies separately, as two distinct actions with no one in supreme tactical command; although the headquarters of the two armies were, when these actions began, not more

than ten miles apart. Each army was successful in its own sphere, but it is probable that success as a whole would have been greater had one mind controlled both. The First Army, for instance, might have cut off the retreat of the Turks who had been defeated by the Third, or vice versa.

But the engagements on the frontier were encounter battles, quite unexpected, and no provision had been made beforehand for the situation which arose.

This mistake was not to be repeated, and to General Demitrieff was assigned the tactical conduct of the battle now in view. I shall come back to this point later.

* * *

The Advance

On the 28th October the general advance was resumed.

The incessant rain which had fallen during the battles of the 22nd–23rd October ceased during the morning of the 24th, and the two days following were fine and bright. On the night of the 26th, however, down came the rain again in torrents, and, although it stopped on the 27th, the roads and tracks were, for the time being, thrown back into the state they had been before the halt. Later the weather cleared again and remained fine until the evening of the 1st November, but the nights were cold.

The Third Army this time advanced not in the echelon formation in which it had marched upon

Kirk Kilisse, but comparatively widely extended in parallel columns, the heads more or less in line.

The valleys and the intervening ridges, running as they do from north to south, afford a series of possible defensive positions at right angles to the general line of advance; and when the Bulgarians started they did not definitely know along which the Turks would be found. Accordingly each division received from the army commander a definite objective upon which to direct its advance, viz:—

5th Division, on the left, upon Bunar Hissar,
4th Division, in the centre, upon Karagach, and
6th Division, on the right, upon Turkbey.

These objectives were 10 to 20 miles, or about a day's march, from the points from which the divisions started.

Each division, then, had from the outset a clearly defined task, to reach a certain place. If the enemy did not intervene, well and good; further objectives could then be allotted. If the enemy did intervene he would straightway be attacked—no waiting for orders or for information in the event of meeting the enemy, because these were the orders, to reach certain places, and so much the worse for any enemy who happened to be, or tried to get, in the way.

One of the two brigades of the 6th Division was detailed as a reserve, to be at the disposal of the army commander if required. This brigade, however, can hardly be called the "general reserve," for in a sense the whole First Army formed, the general reserve.

* * * * *

In the Bulgarian regulations of 1905, in force at any rate a comparatively short time before the outbreak of war, it was clearly laid down that a general or strategical advanced guard should as a rule be employed to cover the march of several divisions advancing to battle. This advanced guard, on obtaining contact with the enemy, was to establish itself on suitable " points d'appui " along a wide front, and was by fighting to obtain for the commander-in-chief both the necessary time and the necessary information to enable him suitably to dispose and deploy the main columns in rear.

It is interesting to note that no attempt was made to put this doctrine into practice. There was no general advanced guard. Each division provided for its own immediate protection; and each marched, more or less independently, upon a distant objective allotted to it by the army commander, making good, one by one, any secondary objectives which happened to intervene. The front covered by the three divisions during this advance amounted to 12 or 15 miles.

Note again the influence of what may be called the de Grandmaison theories as to the protection of large forces and as to their method of advancing to the attack.

Note also that the three divisions of the Third Army (eight brigades) numbered roughly 80,000 men, that is about the equivalent of four divisions of our expeditionary force.

* *
*

The Fighting on the First Day, 28th October.

The 5th Division on the north, having the advantage of the road—the only road,—made more progress on the 28th October than did the other columns, and became engaged with the Turks that afternoon. Its advanced guard reached Bunar Hissar to find this town already occupied, or partly occupied, by the detachment of Bulgarian frontier troops and volunteers, which throughout the advance of the army had protected the extreme left flank, following the Tirnovojik-Samakov road through the Istranja mountains. With their rifles alone this detachment, numbering about 2,000, is said to have succeeded in driving out of the town a whole Turkish regiment (three battalions) and three batteries of mountain artillery. On the arrival of the 5th Division the detachment was sent back into the Istranja, and during the battle it protected the extreme left flank about Sergin.

The Turks, driven out of Bunar Hissar, were followed up to and a little way across the Karagach stream, past the village of Poryali. South-east and north-east of Poryali the top of the ridge is wooded, although the road itself lies along an open clearing. The leading Bulgarian troops appear to have been checked by fire from these woods, and to have been forced to retire back to the right bank of the Karagach stream. The latter flows through a defile here. Both sides of the valley are comparatively steep and of about equal height; neither can be said to dominate the other. The

BATTLE OF LULE BURGAS

woods are sufficiently thick to afford cover from view, but not seriously to impede movement. Backwards and forwards across this valley and through these woods the struggle on the north flank continued for four days.

The central and southern columns were not seriously engaged, if engaged at all, on this, the first, day of the battle. The centre of the 4th Division reached the vicinity of Osmanjik; the centre of the 6th Division the vicinity of Tartarkeui (3 miles west of Turkbey). The advance of both these divisions had been much delayed by the soft state of the tracks.

Third Army headquarters spent the night in Ivankeui; well forward, it will be noticed.

* * * * *

The fighting about Bunar Hissar on the evening of the 28th October, combined perhaps with reports received from other sources, seems to have convinced General Headquarters, back at Kizil Agatch, that the main strength of the Turks was likely to be found upon their right (northern) flank; and that on this flank a counter stroke of some sort might be attempted.

Now the general plan of the battle was with the Third Army to attack the enemy along his front, and with the First Army to envelop his southern flank. The left (north) of the frontal attack was, then, to a certain extent the pivot upon which the enveloping wheel would eventually be made. It would never do to lose this pivot.

The Commander in Chief decided that night that the left (northern) flank of the Third Army, that is the 5th Division, must be reinforced.

The First Army had already started south from about Seliolu towards Lule Burgas on its mission to envelop the Turkish left (south) flank. For the moment then nothing remained at the disposal of the Commander-in-Chief except the one brigade of the 3rd Division (*see page* 52). The reserve brigade of the 3rd Division was on the 28th October at Fikele. In view of the possibility of its being required to reinforce the First or Third Army it had already been ordered to make ground towards the east, and on the morning of the 29th October it reached Achali (6 miles north-west of Seliolu), after an 18 mile march from Fikele. Here it received orders to march at once to reinforce the 5th Division about Bunar Hissar.

Starting again at once, the brigade, accompanied by its vehicles and by three batteries, reached Kirk Kilisse (25 miles) that night, and Bunar Hissar (20 miles) by 5 p.m. the following afternoon, the 30th October, when it moved off at once into action upon the Bulgarian extreme left. This march of over 60 miles in 48 hours along tracks which had in many places become mere swamps—the guns had frequently to be manhandled through the mud—must, as a feat of endurance, almost establish a "record."

It is interesting to note that the news of the arrival of this brigade duly reached Mukhtar Pasha, commanding the Turkish right, who, however, estimated it at a whole division. By the 30th October it is probable that all intercommunication had broken down between the Turkish corps com-

BATTLE OF LULE BURGAS

manders and Abdulla Pasha, and that the latter had ceased in any sense to control the battle. Had this not been the case, had the Turkish troops been suitably disposed, and in communication with each other, and had Abdulla Pasha still maintained some influence on the tactics of the battle—had he, for instance, still possessed any troops in general reserve —it is easy to imagine that the arrival of this Bulgarian brigade, magnified into a division, might have produced even greater tactical results than it actually did. For the news would have gone a long way towards convincing, and perhaps have finally convinced, the Turkish Commander, that the enemy's decisive stroke was about to fall on his right; and he might then have disposed his remaining troops accordingly—whereas in reality the decisive stroke was developing upon his left. The march of the brigade of the 3rd Division, in fact, fitted in well with the reports already furnished to Berlin and the press.

* *
*

The Second Day, the 29th October.

On the 29th October the engagement became general all along the line. Of the actual chronological sequence of events which followed I am a little uncertain.

The 5th Division continued its battle this day east of Bunar Hissar. The 4th Division resumed its advance towards Karagach, which brought it into action on the ridges west of Kulibi. Similarly, the 6th Division continued its advance towards Turkbey, which brought it into action on the ridges west of that place.

Thus, the 4th and 6th Divisions were first engaged on the high ground that lies between the two streams, the Yeno Dere and the Monastir Deresi, the latter being the stream which runs into the Karagach Dere just north of Lule Burgas.

But the Turks were soon driven back across the Yeno Dere; and then from the high ground west of Kulibi and Turkbey, a view must have been obtained of the centre of the main Turkish position 3 to 6 miles away to the east.

* * * * *

The general description of the country given on page 92 applies to the battlefield, and I can think of no part of Europe which resembles it more closely, in a general way, than would Salisbury Plain, if all its little woods and coverts were removed. The Karagach Dere is little more than a trout stream, like the Netheravon; but the only two bridges are at Poryali and Lule Burgas, twenty miles apart.

The main, or the eventual, Turkish position seems to have been intended to run more or less continuously along the left bank of the Karagach Dere as shown on Map No. 4. This bank, exaggerated on the map, is quite a remarkable feature in the landscape; it rises steeply, like a rampart, to an average height of 300 or 400 feet and commands a view towards the west for many miles. A section through the line Osmanjik-Kulibi-Karagach village would, for instance, be roughly as shown on the map. South of

Turkbey, however, its slopes gradually become more and more gentle until, about Lule Burgas, they are considerably less steep than those of the right (western) bank.

The natural instinct of the soldier, especially the untrained soldier, to seek for high ground, to prefer to keep his enemy below him, probably accounts for the selection of this position along the left bank of the Karagach. Tactically I doubt if it was the best available, for, as can be seen from the section, a good deal of dead ground lay along the immediate front; and the more glacis-like slopes of almost any of the other ridges could have been better swept, and therefore defended, by fire—though field of fire is, of course, only one out of many considerations affecting the selection of a defensive position.

The confusion at Turkish headquarters appears to have been so great after the disasters on the frontier that, even with the advantage of four days' grace, it seems doubtful if the available troops were ever allotted to the ground upon any comprehensive and properly thought out scheme of defence. In any case, instead of definitely occupying their main position and improving their very inadequate trenches whilst there was time, some Turkish units—covering troops perhaps—appear to have sallied forth to meet the Bulgarian 4th and 6th Divisions, with the result that the action commenced, as already narrated, along the ridges west of the Yeno Dere. On their left (southern) flank the Turks even crossed the valley and held the hills immediately west of Lule Burgas.

* * * * *

THE CAMPAIGN IN THRACE

THE FRONTAL ATTACK BY THE THIRD ARMY.

The three original objectives allotted to the three divisions of the Third Army were:—

> Bunar Hissar,
> Karagach,
> Turkbey.

Bunar Hissar is seven miles from Karagach: Karagach is five miles from Turkbey. Thus the total length of the frontal attack was originally twelve miles.

Twelve miles are roughly 20,000 yards; that is a front of 20,000 yards was allotted to a force of 80,000 men—four men to a yard, assuming the whole force to be strung out in one line.

Turning to the third paragraph of section 104 of our field service regulations—not a very easy paragraph to understand, but no doubt a very difficult one to write—in which some sort of indication is conveyed as to normal frontages in the attack, we find:—" The general principle is that the enemy must be engaged in sufficient strength to pin him to his ground, and to wear down his power of resistance, while the force allotted to the decisive attack must be as strong as possible. It may be taken that against an enemy of approximately equal fighting value, where the attacking artillery is slightly superior, a force fully equal to that of the enemy holding the position (excluding his probable general reserve) is the least that will suffice for this purpose. Such a force, which should ordinarily be divided into firing line and supports, with local reserves, would be disposed in unequal strength along the front, according to the nature of the ground, the frontage varying from one man to three or more men per yard."

The regulations seem to assume definite knowledge as to the extent of the position about to be attacked—a large assumption—but admit the impossibility of accurately gauging the enemy's strength. For the latter purpose, however, the regulations furnish data for a rough rule in section 108, paragraph 8, where they suggest the allowance of one man per yard for the firing line; of one-fifth to half of that firing line for the supports; and of a number equal to the firing line with its supports for the local reserve.

Applying these rough rules to the Bunar Hissar-Turkbey position, the Bulgarians should have expected to find themselves opposed along that line by about 20,000 Turks in the firing line, plus 10,000 (taking the highest estimate, in support, plus 30,000 in local reserve, i.e. a total of 60,000 men, exclusive of the enemy's probable general reserve.

In attacking the front Bunar Hissar-Turkbey with 80,000 the Bulgarians were, then, well within the limits of the rough indications of our regulations.

* * * * *

But see what happens.

The 5th Division, finding itself held up in the Karagach valley about Poryali, tries to envelop, to outflank the enemy's right; begins to work north towards Sirmos.

Similarly on the southern flank the 6th Division, held up about Turkbey, tries to envelop the enemy's left; a brigade is sent off to attack the hills west of Lule Burgas.

Thus at the end of the first day's fighting the front has become twenty-five instead of twelve miles; instead of four men to a yard the Bulgarians have rather less than two; instead of 60,000 the enemy, if the rough calculation suggested in our regulations be applied, is perhaps 120,000 strong—still excluding his probable general reserve.

* * * * *

How far the higher commanders were responsible for this widening of the front; and how far the troops themselves were compelled to open out by stress of circumstances, obeying a natural instinct to try to go round that which they could not overcome, are not altogether clear. On the north the extension was probably more or less fortuitous, owing to the strength of the frontal opposition. On the south it seems to have been due to the orders of the Army Commander himself.

As already mentioned, at the time when the advance commenced, when the three objectives—Bunar Hissar, Karagach, Turkbey—were originally allotted to the three divisions of the Third Army, there was no certainty of meeting the Turks upon any particular line. They might have been found along the Karagach, or along any other line west or east of the Karagach; or not at all, for they might have been already retiring on Tchatalja. Only the contour, the outpost line had been

BATTLE OF LULE BURGAS 111

ocated; and what was happening behind that line was most uncertain.

When the Third Army met with resistance along the line Bunar Hissar-Turkbey, it soon became obvious that the left flank of the Turks was not at the latter place. From the high ground west of Turkbey, reached on the 29th October, trenches extending south along the Karagach Dere and trenches on the hills west of Lule Burgas could probably have been seen, even if their existence had not been reported beforehand. Thus the situation, as it appeared to the Third Army, was roughly as shown in the diagram below:—

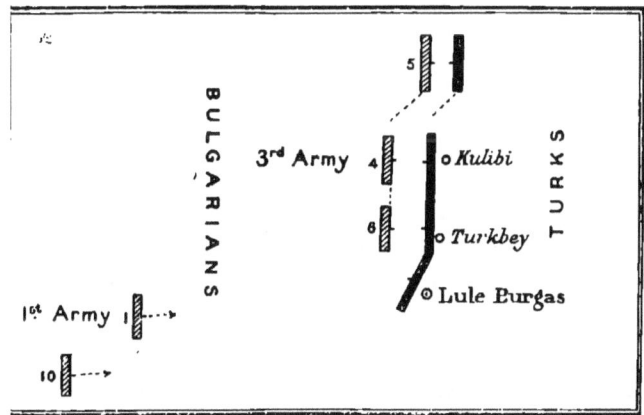

If the whole of the 6th Division continued to advance directly upon Turkbey, then its right flank would be dangerously exposed to the Turks on the hills north-west of Lule Burgas, unless indeed the First Army arrived in time to engage and contain the latter.

But the First Army was late; on the morning

of the 29th October its leading troops were a day's march distant from the battlefield. General Demitrieff therefore decided that the 6th Division must attack *both* Turkbey and Lule Burgas, and he accordingly despatched against the latter place the reserve brigade, the brigade of the 6th Division which he had in the first instance retained at his own disposal.

This brigade succeeded in driving the Turks off the hills west of Lule Burgas, and in the afternoon actually occupied the town, but it is said to have been driven out again in the evening or during the night. The other brigade of the 6th Division, which continued the attack upon Turkbey, appears to have captured that village by nightfall, but to have suffered heavily in crossing the Yeno Dere.

Thus, as the two brigades advanced in divergent directions (the 6th Division consisted of only two brigades), a gap of four or five miles arose between them by the evening of the 29th October. This gap, or rather the isolation of the two brigades at the extremities of the gap and their inability to support each other, caused the Army Commander considerable anxiety until the 1st Division of the First Army eventually arrived upon the scene.

*****

Meanwhile in the centre the 4th Division, after driving the Turks off the high ground west of the Yeno Dere, had some difficulty in forcing a passage across this stream, which was in flood and so deep that a number of men were drowned. An evening

BATTLE OF LULE BURGAS 113

attack, however, enabled the 4th Division to take Kulibi and to make good the watershed between the Yeno and Karagach Deres. Here the troops threw up deep intrenchments—intrenchments which were found invaluable the following morning, for the site was fully exposed to fire and view from the main Turkish position along the commanding left bank of the Karagach Dere.

* * * * *

It is clear that the gap between the two brigades of the 6th Division was not the only gap which arose this day.

The Bulgarian regulations suggest 3,000 yards, or roughly two miles, as a normally suitable frontage for one division in the attack. With the centre of the 5th Division directed on Poryali and the centre of the 4th Division on Karagach—two points eight miles apart—there must obviously have been a gap between the two divisions, if the regulations form any guide at all. And since Karagach is five miles from Turkbey, there must also have been a gap between the right of the 4th Division and the left of the northern brigade of the 6th Division.

And, indeed, there were gaps. By the evening of the 29th October each of the three divisions of the Third Army was practically fighting an isolated action of its own.

Not only were there gaps but there was practically no intercommunication, for it was not until after the battle had fully developed that the signal services were able to complete their chain of field telegraph or telephone lines. In any case, whether intercommunication existed or not, the Army Commander, having sent off his only reserve, had ceased for the time being to have much influence on the conduct of the battle.

All that he could now do was to watch the course of events and to direct the belated columns of the First Army towards the quarter where they were likely to prove most effective.

* * * * *

The situation of the Third Army on the evening of the 29th October and the morning of the 30th seems to have been far from satisfactory. This situation was as follows:—the whole army fully engaged; four separate actions in progress; no reserves in hand; close co-operation practically at an end; the First Army still absent from the battlefield. Against the Turks, untrained, incapable of manœuvre, it mattered little in the long run what were the Bulgarian dispositions; but against active, well-led troops, the outlook would have been serious indeed.

It seems unlikely that the Third Army commander *deliberately* brought about this situation. More probably the situation brought about itself.

What is to be learnt?

In the first place, perhaps, the necessity to study and grasp this question of frontages in battle. Unless commanders and staffs have very clear ideas about the ground and space capacity of their troops, situations similar to that of the Bulgarians on this night of the 29th October seem likely often to arise again. Under modern conditions little will be definitely known of the enemy's dispositions;

for the advance, or the attack, a series of tactical objectives will have to be selected from the map; and unless these objectives are within the capacity of the force attacking them, dangerously wide extensions will result.

Secondly, whatever the original front, the tendency will be, in these long drawn out modern battles, for that front to become wider and wider. Brigades and divisions will not ride straight at their fences; the outer flank men will always try to work round. This tendency, therefore, must be borne in mind in selecting the first objectives.

Conversely, it must be remembered that the enemy's inclination to extend will be no less strong than ours; opportunities may therefore occur of our gaining some advantage from this tendency.

* *
*

ACTION OF THE COMMANDERS.

Having lost control, for the time being, of the operations as a whole, the Army Commander appears to have become engrossed in those of the 4th Division. He spent most of the day, the 29th, on the high ground west of Tashler; and he and his staff attempted at one period directly to supervise the construction of a bridge across the Yeno Dere—with the result that they were caught by surprise artillery fire and were fortunate in escaping without serious loss. The night they passed at Kulibi, within a mile or two, probably, of the advanced trenches of the 4th Division.

* * * * *

116 THE CAMPAIGN IN THRACE

It is interesting to compare the conduct of the two Bulgarian Generals, Savoff and Demitrieff, the former directing the strategy and remaining back at Kizil Agatch, 60–70 miles distant from the point where the decisive battle was now being fought; the latter directing the tactics, and right up in the firing line.

The former was to a certain extent the victim of circumstances. He was responsible for the conduct of the operations, throughout the whole theatre of the war, of three armies and four or five independent detachments. Travelling facilities and means of intercommunication were so primitive that he knew that, if he left Kizil Agatch and tried to get nearer the probable battlefield, he might lose control for a considerable time. When, for instance, general headquarters did eventually, a week after the battle, move forward from Kizil Agatch to Kirk Kilisse, the journey took them two whole days, riding 10–12 hours daily; thus for two whole days the Commander-in-Chief was practically unable either to issue an order or to receive a report. Rather than run the risk which such an interlude would have involved, Savoff decided to remain where he was and to surrender all tactical control to his second-in-command.

*   *   *   *   *

Incidentally it may be noted that what was almost unavoidable in Thrace would not necessarily be advantageous in western Europe. The Commander-in-chief is presumably the best man of his side; the second-in-command the second best.

The big, decisive battle is the most important operation in the whole campaign. It seems, then, neither logical nor sound that the most important operation should be directed by the second-best man, putting into execution not his own general plan, his own ideas, but those of some one else.

Moreover, an alteration in the chain of command generally means improvisation somewhere. The Third Army commander, for instance, might have been unable to command efficiently both his own three divisions and the force as a whole.

* * * * *

If General Savoff went to extremes in one direction, General Demitrieff seems to have gone equally to extremes in another. He was constantly up near the firing line; and during the six days' fighting his headquarters did not spend two consecutive nights in any one place.

" With a small force," say our regulations, " it may be possible to exercise personal supervision, but with very large forces the commander-in-chief should usually be well in rear, beyond the reach of distraction by local events, and in signal communication with his chief subordinates." A force consisting of two armies and a cavalry division, a force of about 150,000 men, must presumably be called a very large force; it is at any rate as large as any force with which our regulations require to deal.

There is this to be said, that by going well forward Demitrieff was able really to *see* a considerable extent of the battlefield, for the panorama was particularly open; standing, for instance,

118 THE CAMPAIGN IN THRACE

on the high ground west of Tashler a view can be obtained in several directions for many miles. Thus the conditions were very different from those of a battle, say, in Surrey, where, if the commander-in-chief goes forward and up and down the firing line, he will seldom see much more than about one company at a time. On the other hand, Demitrieff had neither roads nor motor cars; and the going on horseback was deep.

Some day, perhaps, we shall hear what really was the effect of Demitrieff's ubiquity upon the conduct of this battle.

* *
*

The Sortie from Adrianople

Meanwhile important events were taking place this day round Adrianople. Since the repulse of the sortie on the 22nd of October the 8th Division had securely established itself between the Arda (left bank) and upper Maritza valleys. The 9th Division had taken over all ground west and north-west of the fortress between the Maritza and the Tundja, pushing one brigade across to the left bank of the latter river. And the 3rd Division, now *minus* one brigade which had been sent off towards Bunar Hissar to reinforce the Third Army, was working down south from about Kaipa towards Gebeler and Havsa, and so astride the roads leading to Kirk Kilisse and Lule Burgas. Neither the new 11th Division nor the Servian divisions had arrived; consequently eight Bulgarian brigades, numbering not more than 80,000 men, were extended along the circumference of a circle measuring not less than 50 miles, and were striving to contain a united force, enjoying interior lines, based upon a fortress and numerically not greatly inferior to themselves.

Savoff had in fact concentrated every possible man at the decisive point—the point where the main masses were about to meet; and secondary considerations, of which the investment of Adrianople was one, had for the time being to look after themselves.

* * * * *

Shukri Pasha, the commander of the fortress, being in wireless communication with Constantinople, must have been fairly well acquainted with the general state of affairs. The obvious direction for him to strike a blow was towards the communications of the Bulgarian field armies, or, better still towards the Lule Burgas battle-field itself, distant little more than 40 miles, where he might well have arrived in time to alter the whole history of that struggle. Instead he moved out west.

Why, he will perhaps be able some day to explain. General Ivanoff's staff suggest that he had, perhaps, heard of the near approach down the Maritza valley of certain heavy siege guns, and thought that he might reach and perhaps capture or destroy them before they could reach their destination or be mounted. When great issues were at stake, that at its best could have been but a secondary objective; and it is obvious that a sortie towards Mustafa Pasha, even if successful, could only drive a portion of the investing army back along its communications, and could have little or no effect upon the strategical situation as a whole.

* * * * *

On the morning of the 29th of October two divisions of *nizam* marched out from Adrianople along the left (north), bank of the Maritza, while two regiments of *nizam* supported by some battalions of *redif*, making in all about another division, followed the right bank towards Yurush and Epcheli. The latter met the whole concentrated 8th Division and were easily repulsed. The former made more progress and the engagement which ensued lasted throughout the day.

The Bulgarian line of intrenchments opposite the point of attack of the two *nizam* divisions was held by one brigade of the 9th Division, and ran along the ridge just west of Kemal.

The outposts of this brigade were on the ridge east of Kemal; though not intrenched and within range of the fortress guns, they determined to hold their ground. There was no question of surprise, for the country, although undulating, is open and bare; the Turks marched out in massed formations and in full daylight, and the Bulgarian aeroplanes were making frequent flights. As the outposts refused to retire, they had to be supported from the main bodies in the trenches and with all the available artillery, consisting of one regiment (36 field guns).

The Turks, outnumbering the Bulgarians by more than two to one and supported by the fortress guns, made repeated attempts to storm the ridge, but all their attacks were repulsed. There were no reserves behind the Bulgarian brigade, and it was deemed inadvisable to withdraw troops from any other section of the investing line, so that a counter attack could not have been driven home. Accordingly Sirakoff, the Commander of the 9th Division, received orders to attempt no more than to hold his ground. Late in the afternoon one Bulgarian battery managed to come into action on a spur north-east of Kemal and thence to *rafale* the Turks, who were collecting in a hollow around the little village of Kara Melchu before making another attempt to assault. The losses inflicted by this single battery were so sudden and so heavy—800 bodies were afterwards counted, victims to its shell fire—that the whole Turkish force was thrown into confusion and retreated rapidly back behind the girdle of the forts. The Turkish losses in this sortie amounted to between 1,200 and 1,400 killed.

Thus the 29th October was a critical day, not only for the Third Army but also for the Second.

It is not unlikely that the slow advance of the First Army was dependent on this dual situation, and that General Savoff hesitated definitely to commit his reserve army to any action until it was clear which of the two other armies would most require reinforcement.

It was about this period, probably, that general Headquarters most regretted the absence of the two big detachments, the 7th and 2nd Divisions (*see* page 14).

To return to the main battle.

* *
*

The Third Day, 30th October.

During the 30th October the 5th Division on the north made practically no progress. The local tactical situation was very critical on this flank during this and the following day, for the Turks under Mahmud Mukhtar fought well and with great determination; Poryali, for instance, is said to have changed hands no less than four times in the course of the five days' battle. The situation was partly relieved by the arrival in the evening of reinforcements in the shape of the brigade from the 3rd Division, mentioned above (*see* page 104).

In the centre the 4th Division, finding itself in the open and very much exposed on the ridge east of Kulibi, determined to advance and to storm Karagach village and the heights above it. When exactly this attack took place I am not sure, but before daylight the following morning these objectives had been taken by ten battalions, accompanied by some mountain artillery. The fighting during this incident was perhaps the fiercest throughout the war, and the 4th Division paid a big price for its success. The 8th Primorski Regiment (four battalions) lost 50 per cent. of its strength; of its 16 company commanders 14 were killed or severely wounded, and in one battalion out of 21 officers only one escaped untouched—a solitary survivor, who by the irony of fate died a fortnight later of cholera at Tchataldja.

Of the 6th Division the northern brigade took Turkbey, but failed to cross the Karagach Dere, which, like the Yeno Dere, was in flood and a serious obstacle. However, Taneff, the divisional commander, was told by Demitrieff that, come what may, a crossing must be forced that night. Taneff accordingly placed himself at the head of the brigade and during the night forced a passage and stormed the Turkish trenches upon the opposite bank. Taneff had his horse killed under him, and his aide-de-camp and his divisional flag-carrier were shot dead by his side.

Further south the First Army began to make its presence felt this day. Its leading division, the 1st, seems to have definitely occupied Lule Burgas in the afternoon and then to have started to gain ground slowly up the long glacis-like slopes to the east of the town. The difficulty of finding artillery positions and therefore of providing artillery support is said greatly to have hampered this advance.

On the extreme south the 10th Division, following the Ergene valley, began its envelopment of the Turkish left.

Third Army headquarters spent this night at Ivankeui.

* *
*

The Fourth Day, 31st October.

On the north the 5th Division still made little, if any, progress, although it is probable that the reinforcements, viz:—the brigade of the 3rd Division, began to come into action this day and enabled the turning movement around the extreme Turkish right to develop.

In the centre the 4th Division, having captured

Karagach village and established itself on the commanding left bank of the stream of the same name, began to work north-east towards Tshongara.

Further south the 6th Division, which had succeeded in crossing the Karagach at two points, opposite Turkbey and also near Saranli, gained ground towards the south-east, and during the morning managed to bring artillery into action, about the point marked (A) upon the map, against the flank or rear of the Turkish troops that were engaged with the 1st Division. This fire, combined with the enveloping movement of the 10th Division along the Ergene valley, is said practically to have ended the battle on the southern flank; for all that had hitherto remained staunch of the Turkish left wing then finally gave way and retreated in confusion towards Tchorlu.

The 6th, 1st and 10th Divisions failed, however, to follow up their success; their leading troops halted along or west of the Evrenli Dere.

Demitrieff's headquarters moved south this day and spent the night at Aivali.

* *
*

The Fifth Day, 1st November.

The advance of the 4th and 6th Divisions during the previous day had so completely isolated the Turkish right from the Turkish left that Mahmud Mukhtar's troops were, it seems, not directly or immediately affected by the collapse and retreat

BATTLE OF LULE BURGAS

of their comrades further south. And the fighting on the northern flank continued for at least another day.

The finale on the north was somewhat similar to that on the south. The brigade of the 3rd Division which was working round through the wooded country on the extreme right of the Turks, past Sirmos, managed to bring artillery into action at about the point marked (C) upon the map, and thence to open surprise fire upon Mahmud Mukhtar's reserves, congregated in the valley below, about (R). These were very heavily punished, broke and fled.

About the same time the artillery of the 4th Division succeeded in bringing fire to bear upon the Turkish flank and rear from about (B). The combination of this artillery fire on both flanks with a vigorous attack by the 5th Division in the centre, through the woods north and south of the road, appears to have finally overwhelmed the Turks.

They retreated slowly and in great confusion towards Visa.

During the night of the 1st November down came the rain again in torrents; and although fighting continued around Tshongara and along the Visa road up till about noon of the 2nd November, there was no organized pursuit; nor was Visa itself occupied by the Bulgarians until two days later.

Demitrieff's headquarters spent the night of 1st November at Lule Burgas and that of the 2nd at Yeno.

* *
*

Employment of the Cavalry Division.

The reconnoitring mission allotted to the cavalry division prior to the battle came to end as soon as it could reply to the questions asked; as soon as Nazlumoff could report to the Commander-in-Chief, "the enemy's mass is not there; nor there; but seems likely to be here." That done the Commander-in-Chief had no further need for the cavalry from the strategical point of view and so placed it at General Demitrieff's disposal for employment in the battle.

The orders for the cavalry division then were to co-operate in the tactical operations by working first round and then north against the enemy's left (southern) flank; to make a rather wider sweep but to do more or less what, later, the right brigade of the 6th Division and, later still, the whole First Army, were told to do.

The cavalry appears to have had little difficulty in working round the left flank of the Turks, but to have made little or no progress in their efforts to roll it up. From Turkish accounts of the battle it seems that the Bulgarian cavalry division was opposed by the remnants of the Turkish cavalry corps, and that neither did the other much harm.

The Bulgarian cavalry remained out on this, the southern, flank all through the five days' battle. They occupied Muradli (20 miles south-east of Lule Burgas) at one period but soon left it again; and at some point between Muradli and Seidler they managed to destroy the railway line.

BATTLE OF LULE BURGAS

That seems to be the sum of their successes. But the constant bickering kept them busy and wore out the men and horses just as effectively as if they had been engaged on more important enterprises. Hence it was that when the debâcle came, when first the Turkish left and later their whole line collapsed and retreated in great disorder, the Bulgarian cavalry were found to be stone cold.

Demitrieff issued urgent orders for an immediate and relentless pursuit. Nazlumoff replied that his horses were exhausted and quite unable to move; and he asked for a two days' rest. Demitrieff sent back a message that the brigades might be rested in turn, each for half a day and no more; but how the division could rest its two brigades alternatively and yet remain concentrated is not altogether clear. However, it was no use being angry because the cavalry could not, or would not, and in any case did not, make any important move on either the 31st October or the 1st November; and the heavy rain which then fell helped to put a stop to progress on the 2nd.

* * * * *

Now, General Nazlumoff is a comparatively young officer whose energy and ability earned him such rapid promotion that when I first met him in 1903 he was a regimental commander, whereas when I next met him in 1908 he was Chief of the General Staff. Since then he has been Commandant of the Military School, and, for a year or two before the war, Inspector of Cavalry and commander designate of the cavalry division. Hence it is to be presumed that the Bulgarian cavalry leader knew his work and realized the capacities of his men and horses.

From the time when it started on the 23rd October to pursue the Turks defeated at Seliolu up to the time when the great battle began, the main body of the cavalry division must have marched a distance of little more than sixty miles, or an average of about ten miles per day, including rest days. Consequently, the cavalry ought to have been reasonably fresh when they passed under Demitrieff's command—although, of course, wear and tear of horse-flesh must be measured not in miles but in hours under the saddle.

How could this cavalry best be employed in co-operation with the other arms on the battlefield? That was Demitrieff's problem, and he seems to have sought for a solution in the regulations. "When the cavalry comes into contact with the enemy's infantry," say, or said, the Bulgarian regulations, "it must clear the front, assemble on one or both flanks, and *continue its efforts to penetrate beyond the enemy's first line by the flank.*"

But is this a sound regulation? Was there really much to be gained in this case, for instance, by sending off the cavalry, practically all the available cavalry, away round the Turkish left at the very beginning of the battle?

I think not. Cavalry cannot win battles by themselves; they can only confirm or exploit the victories of the other arms, and to do that they must be in touch, in close co-operation. Of what use cutting or threatening distant lines of retreat before any certainty exists that the enemy intends to use them or, indeed, that he is ever likely to retreat at all ?

Again, and this is perhaps the principal point, cavalry horses carrying seventeen to twenty stone cannot be hunting seven days a week. Their strenuous time comes as a rule during the period *prior* to the battle—as it did here; whilst the First and Third Armies halted, the cavalry reconnoitred. The beginning of the battle should be, as a rule, the time for the cavalry to re-organize and rest; their turn will soon come again. Activity in the cavalry sense does not necessarily mean continuous movement—the cavalry may often be well employed, even though sitting still.

The paragraph in our own regulations which corresponds more or less to that in the Bulgarian regulations quoted above is as follows: " as the opposing forces draw near, the cavalry will be unable to remain in the front line; it will therefore be allotted one or more positions of readiness, where it can best act in accordance with the commander-in-chief's plan, and from which it can easily deploy either to exploit a success gained by the other arms or to support them in case of check." Again, " when a favourable opportunity for cavalry action arises, it must be seized at once; but it is important that the result should promise to have a direct influence upon the decision of the battle, and that cavalry should *not be exposed to heavy losses and horses be exhausted on minor enter-*

prises." It was somewhat upon these latter principles that the Bulgarian cavalry division was employed during the battle of Seliolu, with striking success; and, had similar tactics been put in practice at Lule Burgas, the success might have been renewed.

Demitrieff, however, allotted to the cavalry the task of outflanking the enemy's left, sent his cavalry off upon a practically independent mission at the outset. Hence it seems that upon Demitrieff must fall the responsibility for the very poor results this action attained. The cavalry became exhausted because energy was frittered away upon minor enterprises before the moment for decisive action came.

* * * * *

It must be remembered that the Bulgarian cavalry division at this period cannot have been composed of more than 19-20 squadrons, that is less than 3,000 sabres, or less than 2,000 carbines when dismounted; it included no artillery, having nothing more effective than machine guns. From captured despatches the Bulgarians estimate that 120,000 Turks took part in the actual battle and that about 50,000 more were, and remained, in reserve. Whether, then, such a comparatively puny force of mounted troops could, or could not, have achieved decisive results against a retreating army counting tens of thousands, and including somewhere a cavalry corps which had barely been engaged, must, of course, remain mere speculation.

But military history all tends to prove that

these odds would not necessarily have been too great.

* * *

The Failure of the General Plan.

There was then no pursuit by the cavalry; nor by the infantry; nor by any other arm.

Neither was the Turkish left enveloped; it had gone before the Bulgarian First Army could get round it.

So that the general plan completely failed. Why?

In the first place the timing went wrong. The First Army was late. Its units seem to have had not more than 30–40 miles to march, and yet to have arrived upon the battlefield at least 24 hours after the Third Army had become seriously engaged. The reason has not been revealed, and the whole truth will, perhaps, be never known.

Did the Third Army start too soon? Was Demitrieff in too great a hurry to repeat his successes of Kirk Kilisse? Or did the Turks collapse too quickly, more quickly than the Bulgarian General Staff had dared to hope? Or did the sortie from Adrianople on the 29th October induce Savoff to check the First Army after it had started? Or, again, was it a mere miscalculation of the marching power of the animals and men—march tables upset, perhaps, by the drenching rain which fell on the night of the 26th, probably the very night upon which the operation order for the general advance was issued?

This last was the explanation upon which

General Savoff himself was inclined to lay the greatest stress. The First Army was late because its vehicles were unable to make progress through the mud; the tracks after the rain were in such a terrible state that even in the artillery the horses had to be replaced by teams of oxen. Columns became abnormally long and march discipline was ruined.

Thus it was that the bulk of the leading division, the 1st, only came in for the latter end of the fighting on the Turkish left; while the part played by the 10th Division may be measured by the total of its casualties, which were not more than 25 wounded. And yet both these divisions halted from the 1st to the 5th November no further east than the line of the Evrenli Dere.

Until details are better known it would be rash to draw lessons from the failure of the First Army to fulfil its rôle, except, perhaps, one:—the necessity for practice with these large formations in the field. Practice, and practice alone, will bring home to our commanders the difficulties of marching and manœuvre with bodies (armies) numbering 50–100,000 men, difficulties that are so much greater in reality than they sometimes seem in theory.

The late arrival of the First Army was, then, one reason for the failure both of the envelopment and the pursuit.

* * * * *

What the state of supply of food and ammunition was at the end of the battle I do not know.

Each division maintained its own line of cart

BATTLE OF LULE BURGAS

supply. And the average length of these lines, from railheads in Bulgaria, must have been roughly 100 miles. Railheads had been left on the 17th October; thus about a fortnight had been available for the establishment of intermediate depôts and for putting the system of supply as a whole into working order. But bad weather must, of course, have sadly interfered with all arrangements. The state of supply of the First Army was worse than that of the Third, which had the advantage of extensive captures at Kirk Kilisse.

But it is improbable that lack of supplies was the only, or even the chief, reason for the failure to pursue. A far greater factor was the moral and physical exhaustion of the troops themselves, after continuous fighting and marching for the best part of a week.

General Savoff gave it as his opinion that, under modern conditions, pursuits on a large scale will be carried out only if the commander-in-chief can keep in hand fresh troops for that very purpose. The difficulties of such a course are obvious, for victory must precede pursuit, and only overwhelming superiority could permit troops to be detailed for the latter before the former was assured. In Napoleonic days the case, of course, was different, battles lasting for hours rather than for days and the same troops being able first to fight and then pursue.

* * * * *

Twice, then, in a period of ten days failure to push on, to pursue, lost to the Bulgarians opportunities, or apparent opportunities, of finishing in one month a war which eventually lasted eight, and which cost them, therefore, in lives and money perhaps eight times as much as it need.

The vitally important points for us are first, to discover *why* the pursuit broke down; and next, to see what alterations, if any, we require in our tactics and peace training in order to lessen the probabilities of our failure to pursue when next we win a battle.

* * * * *

I find that the Bulgarian regulations say much the same with regard to the final stages of a battle as do the British regulations. Both agree that the exhaustion, both of personnel and material, at the end of a protracted battle makes a direct, continuous pursuit by the troops who have penetrated the position difficult, if not impossible; involves the necessity of re-organizing a portion of the force at least and of replenishing ammunition and supplies; and calls for great activity on the part of the mounted troops.

With the rôle of the latter I have already dealt. But what of exhaustion? and of the necessity to reorganize?

* * * * *

If it is *exhaustion* which prevents pursuits, and prevents victories being decisive, if exhaustion is such an evil, do we do all possible to try to stave it off? Do our regulations lay enough stress on the importance of husbanding physical energy and strength?

If they do, then why does nearly every battle begin, both in peace training and in war, with an early rise and a long march—or a series of early rises and long marches ?

Often the reasons are obvious. But equally often they are not; and the battle of Lule Burgas is perhaps a case in point, although not such a good example as many which might be quoted. Did the Third Army, for instance, gain as much as it lost by that 15–20 mile march across country, through heavy going, immediately prior to the battle ? Had the Third Army made shorter marches, and economized its strength, would not its men have entered the battle in better fettle, and, incidentally, might not the arrival of the First Army have been more opportune ?

"Time lost can never be regained," we say—and remember. We forget, perhaps, that human energy once expended can be recovered only by a rest ; and that the fresher the troops on entering battle the longer they will last.

"La perte du temps," wrote Napoleon to his brother, " est irréparable à la guerre ; les raisons que l'on allègue sont toujours mauvaises, car les opérations ne manquent que par des retards." That, no doubt, is true. But time is not saved by long marching only. Hesitation, weak-mindedness, want of definite, determined plans are equally potent factors and it was, perhaps, rather to these that Napoleon referred.

* * * * *

Habit has probably much to do with early rising and long marching prior to a battle. In the operations of peace training a great many events have to be crowded into a short space of time ; the troops must start fighting at the earliest possible moment or there will not be time to fight at all; army manœuvres must be begun and ended in four days. Therefore, we rise early and march far before we fight in peace; we form the habit of so doing and then we do so in war. But the advantages and disadvantages might often be weighed more carefully than they are. Frequently it is a race for ground; but the action which follows the race, and not the immediate result of the race itself, is likely to decide the battle.

It is interesting to note that our regulations of 1905, written when the lessons of the South African war were comparatively vivid, laid stress on the evils of early marching. "In fixing the hour of starting the comfort of the troops should, as far as tactical exigencies admit, be considered. Both men and horses obtain most rest in the early hours, whilst it is always advisable that men should have their breakfasts, and animals be fed before starting; this is particularly the case when grazing is depended upon, as animals graze more freely in the morning. When practicable, therefore, the hour for starting should not usually be before daylight."[1] That paragraph, or its equivalent, will not be found in our revised regulations of 1912.

* * * * *

So much for exhaustion. Next what of *re-organization after a battle*? and the intervention of the mounted troops in the final stages?

Partly because time is always limited and because

[1] *Combined Training*, 1905, Section 18.

we nearly always begin at the beginning—the reconnaissance and approach march stage—and partly because the sides are generally of approximately equal strength, we rarely arrive at the final stages in our peace manœuvre battles. A deadlock is reached before either side is prepared to acknowledge the necessity to retire. Thus the exhaustion or the absence of the mounted troops is seldom realized; " cease fire " sounds before the latter are called upon to intervene. And reorganization of the remainder takes the form of a rally *to the rear*— back to the camps or bivouacs of the night before, —under peace conditions.

Is that the best possible preparation for this most difficult phase in war?

* * * * *

Unless we can devise manœuvre schemes which will involve systematic practice of these final stages of a modern battle, of re-organization and pursuit, it seems unlikely that we shall do any better than did the Bulgarians after their victory at Lule Burgas—Bunar Hissar.

There must be a muddle at the end of every battle, just as great a muddle in war as in peace manœuvres. In fact, in large scale modern battles there must often be a period when the confusion is so great that none of the actors really know which side is winning or which side has lost—nobody knows the *total* score all along a line, 25, 50, or 100 miles long. If that is so, then there must often be a period when the result hangs in the balance, when those who can be made to *think* that they are winning will win; and those who think that they are losing will be lost—whatever be the real state of affairs as a whole.

Then, the side which can extricate itself from that confusion best and quickest, which can re-organize without prolonged halting or, worse still, marching to the rear, that surely is the side most likely to win.

But how can commanders, staffs and troops learn to extricate themselves from confusion, to rally and re-organize *forwards, on a large scale*, if the problem is rarely practised, if the solution is so seldom sought in peace training ?

In nine cases out of ten, when the confusion of the peace battle becomes or threatens to become really confounded, the situation is ended by the " dismiss " and the " officer's call." That is an easy solution, but one of no practical value for war. Unless we get well into deep water frequently we shall never learn to swim with ease.

* *
*

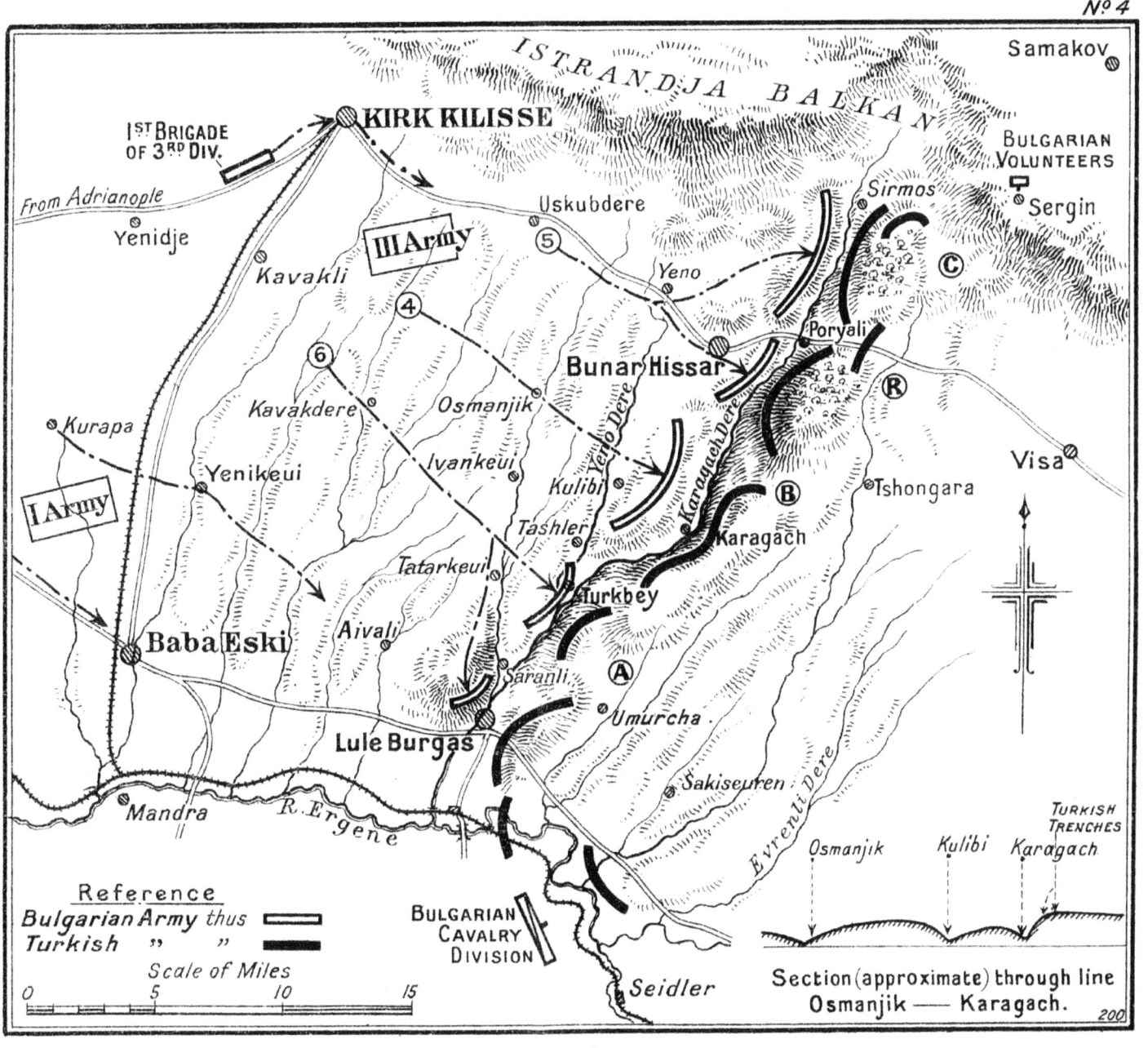

SIXTH LECTURE

NOTES AND COMMENTS

EXCEPTING some minor operations which ended in the capture of Yaver Pasha and his division at Marhanli, about twenty miles northeast of Dedeagatch, the battle of Lule Burgas-Bunar Hissar may be said to have finished the manœuvre phase of the campaign of 1912.

Further operations in Thrace resolved themselves, for all practical purposes, into two sieges—of Constantinople, defended by the Tchatalja Lines, and of Adrianople.

Siege operations are of tactical, rather than strategical, interest and to study tactics with profit far more details are required than I was able to collect, and far more than have appeared as yet in any publication. I therefore leave these operations until some day details may be available; and I conclude with a few miscellaneous notes and comments.

* * * * *

It may be said, and with some justice, that until *full* details are known no conclusions of any sort should be drawn from any war. Such a policy is, perhaps, the safest, but not necessarily the soundest from the soldier's point of view. For two reasons.

Firstly, however long he waits a completely truthful history will never appear, for military operations do not lend themselves to accurate description. Personal experiences of even the same episodes are often totally at variance. Take, for instance, the ordinary peace manœuvres of any army. They are watched and recorded by staffs of directors, umpires and narrative officers, by privileged spectators and uncensored and uncontrolled correspondents of the press—and yet when the reports are published few of the actors agree that the description of events is altogether accurate, or the comments altogether fair.

Military history is at its best but a compromise between a number of conflicting opinions and facts; and the histories of this Balkan war are likely to prove particularly untrustworthy and, perhaps, misleading. The Turks will publish next to nothing. The Allies will let the world know as much as suits them, and no more. They are under no obligation to educate the armies of other nations; nor is it to their interest to share their lessons with the world at large. Herein lies one objection to deferring any study of this, the latest, war.

The other reason is that soldiers must learn such lessons as they can when and while they may. The process of keeping up to date with modern military developements must always be more or less a hand-to-mouth business; for no soldier can with any certainty foresee whose turn it will be next to enter the ring.

On the whole, then, it seems to me unsound to

defer reading, talking or thinking about this war until the official publications appear to tell us what to say and think.

* *
*

What is the special value of the war?

It is the latest war, of course, and the latest war has always a special value of its own—until the next war takes its place.

But, though the latest war, it cannot in every sense be classed as *modern*; only to a limited extent can it convey to us an impression of what modern European warfare really means. The armament was up to date; but, as in Manchuria, the general state of the country, in which all the operations took place, was a hundred or five hundred years behind the times.

We can learn, then, little or nothing as to the influence upon future wars of the material factors of modern civilization; of the network, for instance, of roads, railways, telegraphs, telephones, wire fences and enclosures which cover the surface of western Europe, of dependence of the vast civil populations on imported food, or of the gigantic strides made in the development of motor and mechanical transport.

The tendency is, perhaps, to exaggerate these external influences; for wars or, at any rate, battles —and the battles decide the wars—soon work down in practice to a brutal, semi-savage struggle of man against man. However, this Balkan war helps us very little to decide whether such influences are made too much of or too little realized.

* * * * *

For us there seems to me to be special value in the war from two points of view. Firstly, it was a war in which one side was practically untrained; secondly, it was a colonial war—or what we usually call a " small " or " colonial " war, for want of a better word.

* * * * *

A number of people are busy drawing comparisons between our own military institutions and those of the Turks. So I will not dwell on this aspect of the war; except to say that no army could be found, in Europe at any rate, *more* closely resembling the Turkish army, in some respects, than do the territorial armies of the United Kingdom and our Colonies.

Whether that fact matters or not is a question for others to decide. But there the fact is. And, if as soldiers we face the fact rather than merely bemoan it, then a great deal may be learnt from the misfortunes of the Turks. We may learn, for instance, what strategy and tactics are, or are not, suitable for gallant troops, inadequately organized and trained ; for troops whose standard of efficiency is lower than that of their opponent.

No one can say that the Turks made the most of such means as they possessed. How in somewhat similar circumstances should we make sure of doing better ?

* * * * *

Looking upon the campaign in Thrace as a colonial campaign, as a war fought for instance under Asiatic rather than European conditions, a great many useful lessons may be learnt.

For purely academic purposes take, for instance, Afghanistan. Afghanistan is one of our bogeys; a potential enemy—all foreign states with whom we have a common frontier must be so, however friendly existing relations may be.

In organization, armament, training and efficiency the Afghan army bears some resemblance to that of the Turks. Racial and religious characteristics of the two peoples are not unlike; the oriental qualities of fanaticism, inertia, supineness, stolidity tempered by guile, are more or less common to them both. Topographical and climatic conditions are not dissimilar; the resources of Thrace are little more developed than those of Afghanistan; communications, customs, habitations are in much the same primitive stage.

The comparison must not be carried too far; but, if war either with or in Afghanistan ever became inevitable, we might with profit follow in some respects the example of the Bulgarian General Staff.

We might, for instance, take full advantage of Afghan lethargy and lack of system; select the time, occasion, season which happened to suit us best; and catch the Afghans as little prepared, and as much by surprise, as the Bulgars caught the Turks.

Such a policy would mean close co-operation between the authorities responsible for foreign politics and war; rigid censorship and blockade of the frontier; mobilization and concentration kept as far as possible secret; and no ultimatum or declaration of war until our forces were ready to move.

Again, we might march troops across country hitherto supposed to be impassable. There was probably in Bulgaria before the war a party which considered an invasion of Thrace as possible only along hitherto recognized routes; and a party which said that an army of two to three hundred thousand men could never be fed or supplied without a railway; that an army of such a size could never manœuvre at a distance of more than two or three days' march from its bases and railheads.

And yet these things have happened.

Similarly, are we not a little inclined, when considering possible operations on or beyond the north-west frontier of India, to exaggerate the difficulties of terrain? to concentrate attention on the historical lines of advance into Afghanistan to the exclusion of all others? to allow difficulties of supply to loom a little too large? and to call railway construction essential when, perhaps, it is not really so?

Marshal Soult's opinion on this point is worthy of note. Soult was on active service almost continuously for some twenty-five years, before railways were invented, when natural obstacles were no easier than they are to-day, and when men and animals marched no better than they now march and required just as much to eat.

Writing of frontiers he says, "And yet these difficulties were never insurmountable, even when taken as a point in the line of defence. Some issue invariably left ignored, some difficult pass left to be discovered, afforded the means of a passage to obtain another and a better one. The first point gained left others won or compromised, and there is no example of an army which made any *serious* attempt having failed."

That, perhaps, is a slight exaggeration; but, without any doubt, it is the unexpected, or the apparently impossible, which so often succeeds in war.

Therefore, from the defensive point of view we must budget for the unexpected; and from the offensive point of view we must often contemplate the apparently impossible.

And in reply to those who say that large armies cannot cross the Indian frontier, or the English Channel, or that even if they do cross them they will assuredly be starved—in reply we can point to the Bulgarian invasion of Thrace.

* * *

Except that it had few if any aeroplanes— and who knows with any certainty which side will have, and will *retain*, air craft in future wars —except that it had no properly organized flying corps, and that it was short of cavalry, few armies have gone to war possessing greater facilities for the collection of intelligence than did the Bulgarian army when the campaign opened.

A friendly population, including well-organized revolutionary societies and bands; swarms of deserters and refugees arriving daily in their camps; the area of operations open, easily reconnoitred and observed.

And yet as soon as the frontier was crossed the *fog of war* came down as thick as ever.

All sources of information seemed to close directly the respective forces began to come in contact. There resulted unforeseen, unexpected encounter battles on the frontier; great victories won but not fully realized; and, finally, such confusion that for three or four whole days a halt was called until the new situation could be grasped and a fresh start organized.

* * * * *

Now the general plan of campaign was nothing if not simple, and elastic enough to cover several possible contingencies. Kirk Kilisse was first to be taken, and then the main hostile mass attacked—the sooner the better.

And yet there was that pause, that temporary failure consistently to keep the ball, once started, rolling. The plan did not fail; it was eventually carried through; but the delay in its execution enabled the Turks partially to recover from their preliminary disasters.

If the reason for the Bulgarian hesitation could definitely be fathomed, we might learn some useful lessons.

Anxiety to avoid disorder was probably one reason; for the pursuit of an enemy in disorder must always involve more or less disorder amongst the troops pursuing.

Unwillingness to get committed to a wrong direction, another reason.

Difficulties of supply, a third.

But not one of these three reasons, nor even their combination, need necessarily have been decisive.

Because only portions, not the whole, of the invading armies were engaged in the battles on the frontier—the remainder were fresh and in hand. The directions taken by the pursuing columns, within certain limits, did not matter, for the vanquished must almost always adjust their dispositions to those of the victors. And problems of supply should not have been insoluble, in view of the quantity of captured stores, and of the comparative proximity of the Bulgarian armies to their bases at the time.

Had, then, the advance continued immediately after the victories of the 22nd and 23rd October, had the general plan been carried through without a check, there seems no reason to suppose that it would have failed in the execution; and every reason to suppose that the final success would have been infinitely more striking than it eventually proved to be.

* * * * *

To me it appears far more likely that the thickness of the fog of war rather than any other factor accounted for the check.

The commander and staff at General Headquarters were expecting to know too much; were relying upon receiving more perfect and more timely information than we must expect to receive in war. Then, when this information failed to come, or when its general tenor was completely different to what had been expected, they were surprised; their mental equilibrium was temporarily upset, their plans were temporarily thrown out of gear.

They had worked out their scheme repeatedly in theory. They had quite decided that the capture of Kirk Kilisse must involve operations lasting at least for several days. During that period there would be time to get back information from further afield; time to digest it, to pass it round, and then to write orders for the second stage.

But in practice events moved with wholly unforeseen celerity, and General Headquarters failed to keep pace with the times. The kaleidoscopic changes were so rapid that " appreciations of the situations " and the issue of orders, based upon them, ceased, as fast as they were written, to suit actual circumstances. Items of information which were received were hopelessly out of date before they arrived. The operations ran away, so to speak, from the scheme, and General Headquarters were normally dealing with " narrative No. 3 " whilst the troops were already in the middle of " narrative No. 5." Until at last, in despair, General Headquarters sounded halt.

They were working too much upon preconceived ideas, and had not made enough allowance for this fog of war.

* * * * *

What are the lessons ?

The danger of preconceived ideas.

The necessity to practise with obscure situations, so that when we get into the fog we shall not lose our heads.

The necessity to realize that timely information will often be lacking in war.

The necessity to devise *and adhere to* simple, straightforward, reasonably elastic plans; the latter based upon our own requirements, aims, intentions and not upon news of the enemy.

The necessity to foresee, forestall the most unlikely turns of events, and to have suitable alternative plans thought out; and even, perhaps, to have orders for their execution ready drafted—for it is the *promulgation* of big decisions, involving great changes, not necessarily the arrival at the big decisions, which so often means the loss of precious time. The staff must insure against loss of time, when time is really precious, by spending beforehand plenty of time, when time is cheap.

* * * * *

But for whom are these lessons most essential? For the higher commanders and their staffs.

They are all lessons relating to the *art of command*, the chief command of the force whatever it be.

This being so, it seems unfortunate that under existing conditions the opportunities of obtaining practice in the exercise of command, either in field manœuvres or in theoretical exercises, are in inverse ratio to the size of the unit, or the rank of the commander concerned.

Squadron and company commanders, for instance, are actually exercised in their capacity to command their units more regularly and frequently than regimental and brigade commanders; regimental and brigade commanders more regularly and frequently than divisional commanders. An army commander rarely commands an army more than once, or at most twice, during the period he is earmarked for such a responsible appointment in the event of war.

The higher the rank attained the less the opportunities of practice in command. That is the rule.

And yet the larger the unit the more difficult it is to exercise command efficiently, and the more important are the issues involved.

The further we advance up the ladder of promotion, the more often we direct, supervise, stage-manage, instruct, inspect or take the place of referee; the more often we *set* problems in the art of command, the less often do we actually *solve* them.

And yet it is from the solving, not from the setting, of the problems that practice is gained. The man who has constantly to face the fog of imaginary war is the man who is making progress, not the man who merely creates that fog by compiling a suitable scheme. Neither the setting of the scheme nor the criticism of its execution need call for much effort of mind or will.

But without such effort where is the profit? How can the powers of thought and will be improved except by being exercised?

Speaking generally, our system of peace training is such that the imaginative and critical faculties of our leaders are being developed to a relatively greater degree than are those of reasoning and resolution.

That is a bold indictment but it seems to me to be a true one.

* * * * *

Our training regulations are perhaps a little to blame. The overwhelming importance of constant practice in *command* is not definitely laid down. The regulations hold commanders responsible for the training and efficiency of their *units*, but make no mention of their responsibility towards *themselves*; with the result that higher commanders too readily adopt the passive rôle of inspector, director or umpire, and too rarely that of leader.

Better co-operation in the arrangement of training programmes might create more opportunities for the higher commanders to command. A brigadier, for instance, might more often command his brigade in a scheme set and directed for him by a fellow brigadier.

But the first essential is to part with prevailing notions that the efficiency of the leader is relatively of less importance than the efficiency of the led; that actually to command one side in peace training operations is a less important, less dignified rôle than to remain neutral and watch, direct or inspect the operations of both sides; that exercises must necessarily be criticized adversely; and that such criticism, if called for from a junior on the action of his senior, necessarily implies lack of respect.

152 THE CAMPAIGN IN THRACE

Criticism at its best is but a matter of opinion, and, if well reasoned and sound, why should the most senior amongst us be unwilling to accept his share ?

Discipline must be weak indeed if a little honest criticism is liable to break its bonds.

* * *

The high standard attained by the Bulgarians in military organization, leadership and general efficiency is perhaps the most striking feature of the war. Thirty-five years ago Bulgaria, as a state, had not so much as begun to exist. Her development as a military power is, in fact, more remarkable, rapid and romantic than even that of Japan.

An army, a highly successful army, has been created *ab ovo* in one generation — within the lifetime of most of us here. The history of the evolution of that army is well worth careful study. I can only attempt to give the merest outline, and to pick out a few of the prominent points.

* * * * *

A Bulgarian contingent, that is a body of some 10,000 peasant volunteers, led by Russian officers, fought, and fought well, alongside the Russians in 1877. When, after that war, the Principality of Bulgaria was established, this contingent formed the nucleus of its army; but Russian officers continued to fill all appointments of higher than subaltern rank. The new national forces soon proved their worth, for the revolt in Eastern

Roumelia, in 1885, led to a concentration of Turkish troops in the neighbourhood of Adrianople, and the Bulgarians gathered east of Philippopolis to meet them. At this critical moment all the Russian officers were suddenly withdrawn; and the Servian army marched on Sofia. Nothing daunted, the Bulgarians, led by their subaltern officers (the generals of to-day), turned west and by some extraordinary feats of marching reached Sofia before the invaders, defeated them at Slivnitza, and drove them back on Nish, only Austrian intervention preventing further progress.

The records of that short campaign are of great interest, but, to the best of my knowledge, there is only one book, in English, dealing with the subject.[1]

* * * * *

Since 1885 there has not been a single foreign officer in Bulgarian employment. A considerable number of Bulgarian officers have, it is true, graduated at foreign staff colleges, but with no marked partiality; to any school prepared to welcome them Bulgarian officers have been sent, and those of Italy, Russia, Austria, France and Belgium have all been visited in turn.

Thus, organization and training have developed on independent and national lines; and advantage has been taken, throughout that development, of the teaching and experiences not of one nation but of many. The Bulgarians, in fact, have had

[1] *The Struggle of the Bulgarians for National Independence under Prince Alexander.* Translated from the German of Major A. von Huhn, 1886.

war—war of a particular kind, a calculable campaign against a predetermined enemy—staring them in the face from the time when they first began to mould their army; and being eminently practical people, they have moulded it to suit their own requirements, and not to accord with the theories or doctrines of others.

* * * * *

Particular attention was paid to the lessons of the Russo-Japanese War. The Bulgarians recognized a certain similarity between the problem which lay before them in the Balkans and that which had faced the Japanese in Manchuria. Accordingly, the military successes of the latter were studied with great interest, and no time was lost in adopting certain features of the Japanese organization which had in actual practice definitely proved their worth—notably the organization of the Japanese General Staff.

The Bulgarian General Staff, like that of the Japanese, is a *distinct corps*. Once finally selected for the General Staff the officer remains a member of it, and wears its special aiguillette and buttons, until promoted to the command of a regiment or a brigade. The General Staff officer gets little more pay than other officers, but he gets more rapid promotion, and, consequently, competition to enter the General Staff is very great. The series of tests are, however, most exacting, and of these the *p.s.c.* diploma is only an initial step. Just before the war began a Staff College was opened in Bulgaria itself, but, up till then, all competitors had to obtain their diplomas at one of the Staff Colleges of certain foreign armies.

General Savoff, for instance, graduated at St. Petersburg, General Fitcheff at Milan, whilst on the Headquarter Staff during the war were representatives of at least three other military schools.

This fact, it might seem, would tend to divergence of opinions and to lack of a common doctrine, but such, I was assured, was not the case. And for two reasons. Firstly, the instruction given at the staff colleges of all the leading military nations is, in the long run, much the same—we all study the same subjects and all in much the same way. Secondly, the staff college course is the mere introduction and not the finale of a Bulgarian staff officer's education. Five years' further training follows before it is possible for his name to be enrolled finally in the special corps.

The institution of the latter, it is claimed, has proved a great success; largely because it has solved most of the difficulties of giving accelerated promotion, and those of providing for each officer practical experience with arms other than his own. The Bulgarian General Staff officer returns to regimental duty for two years before each step in rank, and on these occasions he is posted, as an *executive* officer, to each of the arms in turn. He thus obtains, in time, a thorough insight into the practical working of *all three arms*; and without that thorough insight, so the Bulgarians maintain, no commander, and no staff officer, can be fully qualified to issue orders to a force composed of all three arms.

Many Bulgarian officers expressed the opinion that it was in the art of command and in staff work that their chief superiority over the Turks lay. In fact, they attribute their victories very largely to the excellence of their commanders and their staffs; and the excellence of these to the system upon which they are brought up.

During the war the commander of practically every unit larger than a regiment (a Bulgarian regiment corresponds, roughly, with a British brigade) was an ex-officer of the General Staff.

* * * * *

The peace organization of the Headquarter Staff at Sofia corresponds very closely with the war organization; so that the war staff can often be exercised as such in time of peace, and upon mobilization very few changes of personnel need occur.

Compared with our own, the Bulgarian staffs are small. For instance, only twelve General Staff officers actually accompanied the Commander-in-Chief in the field, viz. :—

the chief of the General Staff (Major-General),
the sub-chief of the General Staff (Colonel),
four officers of the Operations Section,
four officers of the Information Section, and
two officers of the Communications, or Railway, Section.

With these, and with a correspondingly small staff of administrative officers, General Savoff succeeded in controlling the operations of three armies, two independent divisions, the cavalry

NOTES AND COMMENTS 157

division and a number of detachments—in all a force of about 400,000 men.

To each of the staffs of the three armies in the field only six General Staff officers were allotted.

The business-like simplicity with which these comparatively small staffs seemed capable of coping with their work, both at general headquarters and at the headquarters of the armies, is worthy of note.

* * *

The *moral and psychological* side of the science of war receives at least as great attention in Bulgaria as in Japan. Patriotism is deliberately cultivated, not left to take its chance. The men in the ranks, for instance, are all taught to sing patriotic songs, and a company on the march seemed to be more often singing than silent, the ranks or sections taking each a verse in turn.

Bands are not broken up on mobilization, but accompany their units in the field. During the assaults on Petra and on Karagach the bands, for instance, were playing the National Anthem.

Nor are regimental colours considered to be out of date in modern war. During several of the more critical periods of the battle of Lule Burgas-Bunar Hissar regimental commanders themselves, I was told, actually carried their own standards.

* * * * *

Bayonet fighting seems to have been quite a feature of the war.

It has been suggested that the fierce feelings of

racial and religious hatred, common to both sides, were responsible for a blind striving of each to reach the other with cold steel. That explanation is not, I think, the true one. As a race, the Bulgarians are essentially cool-headed and phlegmatic, and I rarely heard, either on this occasion or on any other, deep feelings of personal animosity expressed against the Turks, however gross the provocation. Members of the other Christian races in the Balkans make little secret of their abomination of the Turk, but the Bulgarians more often seem disposed to treat him as a joke.

Peace training rather than a disposition to " see red " accounts for the use of the bayonet in this war.

Like the Japanese, the Bulgarians have made a fetish of the bayonet. Bayonet fighting had been practised every day ; during their drills the infantry soldiers had constantly been made to charge dummies and actually to transfix them with their bayonets ; every tactical exercise had ended with a bayonet attack, and the men had always been made to charge through and beyond each other— not to halt at a distance of 50 yards, as laid down in our training regulations. Regulations forbidding bayonets to be fixed, or swords drawn, in peace exercises where there are opposing forces, and forbidding any actual contact, are, in the opinion of the Bulgarian General Staff, regulations likely to do more harm than good. Thought and theory all go to the winds, they maintain, in the final stages of a modern battle, after the prolonged strain of the preliminary phases ; and men remember then only what they know so thoroughly as to be able to do it *without thinking*, force of habit, and not reasoning power, becomes the dominating factor.

Before the war, the Bulgarians themselves had begun to consider that bayonet work and long hours of humdrum drill were being rather overdone, and an agitation had arisen for reform. That agitation has now completely disappeared.

According to the Bulgarian regulations, bayonets were supposed to be fixed on reaching a distance of 600 yards from the enemy. After the first week or two of the war the custom arose of keeping bayonets practically permanently fixed. During the month I spent in Thrace, I rarely saw, except inside a railway truck, a rifle without its bayonet. The rank and file were all in favour of the change and in fact had evolved the habit largely for themselves. The officers, too, maintained that their men thereby became accustomed to the weight and balance of the rifle with its bayonet fixed, and also that their musketry had improved. The Turks, who did not fix bayonets till the last possible moment, invariably fired high; but the weight of the bayonet at the end of the rifle helped to counteract a similar tendency on the part of the Bulgarians. Again, with bayonets permanently fixed, there was no danger of being surprised in a hand-to-hand combat or of forgetting to fix them until too late. Instances were quoted to me of the Turks being caught defenceless when the final encounter took place—unable to draw and fix their bayonets in time.

THE CAMPAIGN IN THRACE

Before the war there had been an outcry for longer bayonets, to put the Bulgarian infantry on terms of equality with the Turkish. Although the respective advantages of the short and long bayonet had not been definitely decided, most of my informants had, they said, changed their minds, and were now in favour of the short bayonet. The latter, being lighter, is more easily handled, is less fragile, and more easily withdrawn from the adversary's body after a successful lunge. Great stress was laid on the necessity to keep the points of the bayonet sharp and to insist upon a strong attachment. It was often found difficult to drive a blunt sword bayonet through the greatcoats and equipment of the Turks; and in hand-to-hand fighting cases occurred of bayonets becoming accidentally detached.

Most of the bayonet fighting is said to have taken place at dusk or by night. But there were instances of bayonet encounters even by day, for instance, when the 1st Division captured certain Turkish trenches near the town of Lule Burgas.

* * * * *

Attacks at dusk, as opposed to night attacks or attacks at dawn, are said to have been another special feature of the war. Fire would be concentrated upon a certain point, usually a flank, during the late afternoon, and an assault with the bayonet would be made as soon as approaching darkness began to put an end to aimed fire. Positions so captured would be entrenched and held, and little attempt made to follow the retreating Turks to any great distance beyond the original objective.

How far this system of evening attacks had been

practised in peace, and how far evolved during the campaign, I do not know. The advantages claimed are :—(a) that directions and formations are less liable to be lost than they are in a night attack, for objectives can be clearly indicated and each individual can mark his point and run for it just before the light altogether fails; (b) that previous fire preparation and support is not wasted, for the attack with the bayonet follows closely on the attack by concentrated fire; and (c) that, if the attack is successful, the men are likely to get a comparatively good night's rest, for the action is over about an hour after dark.

* * *

Of the two adversaries the Turks, on the whole, were the better armed, equipped and clothed, at the beginning of the war.

At the time of my visit quite a number of Bulgarian soldiers could be seen carrying or wearing captured Turkish arms or equipment in preference to their own. This point has been disputed and a great deal of nonsense has been written, for instance, concerning the so-called superiority of the Schneider-Creusot gun, with which the Bulgarian first-line artillery is armed, over the Krupp gun possessed by the Turks. The superiority lay in the employment of the gun and not in the gun itself. In fact, quite a number of Bulgarian artillery officers informed me that on the whole they preferred the Krupp guns to the Creusot.

Officers of the General Staff took a very broad view of this matter. All modern guns, rifles and equipment are, they maintained, for practical purposes very much the same; and a great deal of energy, time and money gets wasted, in all armies every year, in searching for perfection or in striving to go one better than one's rival. Perfection should be sought for, and superiority attained, not in the implement but in the use to which it is put.

The Turkish gunners, they said, obviously knew next to nothing about ranging, fuse-setting, or the observation, control, concentration and distribution of fire. Those, for instance, in the Adrianople batteries did not know even the ranges of prominent points within a few thousand yards of their forts, and were in the habit of firing wildly at anything they saw.

The Bulgarians, on the other hand, pride themselves on the efficiency of their artillery personnel. Quite a number of instances occurred where single batteries or regiments of artillery, working well forward during the course of an engagement, succeeded, as in the action of Kemal (see page 121; see also pages 70, 124 and 125), in bringing surprise fire to bear upon bodies of Turks in mass or close column formations, with decisive results. But successful *coups* of this sort were due entirely to the initiative and skill of the gunners and in no way to the quality of their guns or shell.

* *
*

Both sides dug freely.

In the Bulgarian armies it appears to have been a more or less regular rule for the leading troops to entrench themselves, whenever halted, whether in close touch with the enemy or not; and the quality of their trench work was, as a rule, well up to the standard of the text books.

The entrenching of the Turks, upon the contrary, was beneath contempt. They seem to have lacked the most elementary knowledge as to the proper siting of trenches, which were often so placed on the crests of the slopes that, whilst fully exposed themselves, their own field of fire was limited to a dozen yards. Companies and battalions in some cases entrenched in a mass or column formation, one trench immediately behind the other. Continuous trench work was rare; each man, as a rule, dug for himself a crude, oblong pit in which he lay with his legs as high as, and sometimes higher than, his head, whilst the front parapet was often so thin as to be easily knocked away to nothing by a single kick.

It would not be easy to find the difference between the work of well-trained and untrained troops more clearly accentuated than amongst the labyrinth of trench work which still outlines the battlefields of Thrace.

* * *

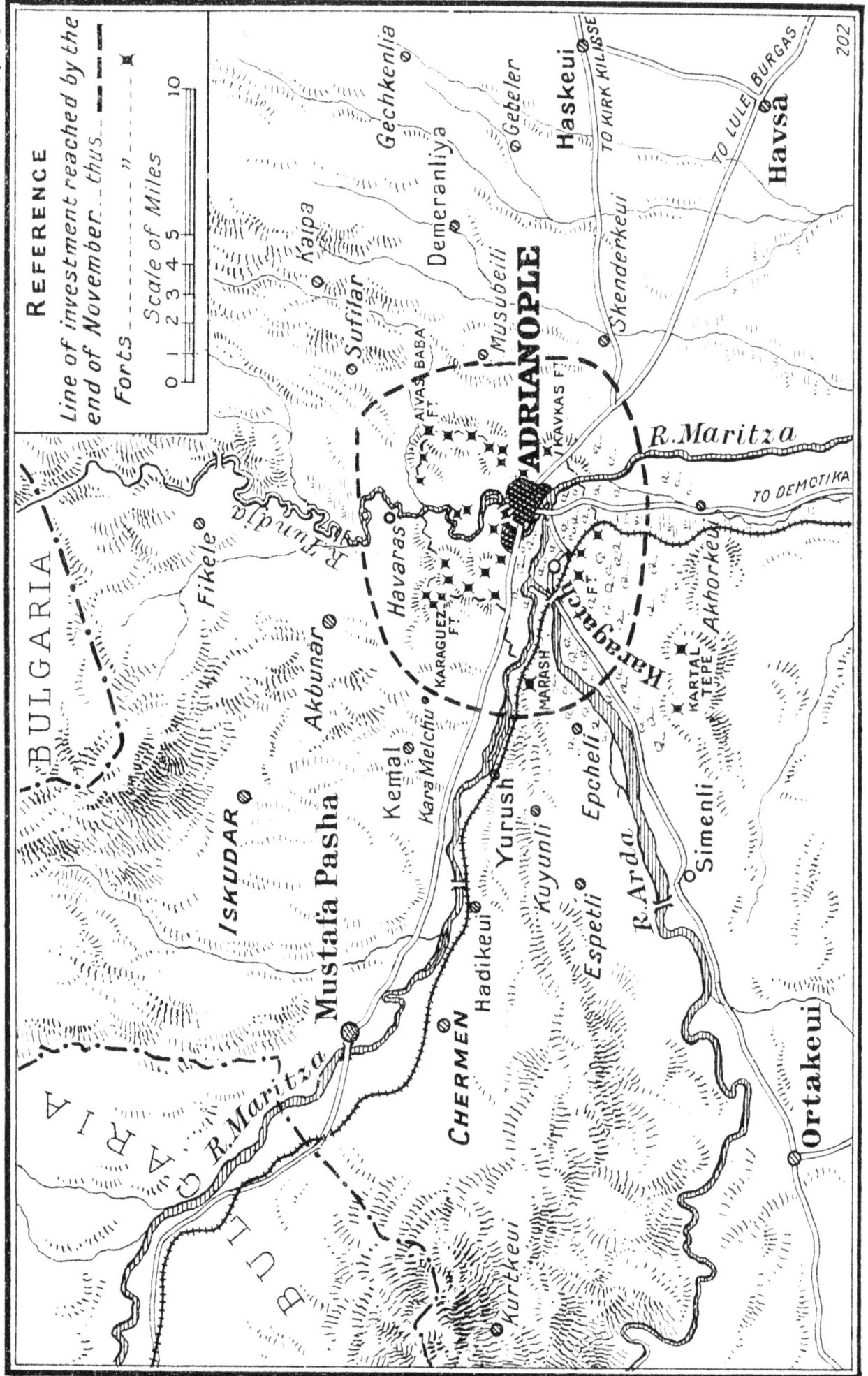

www.ingramcontent.com/pod-product-compliance
Lightning Source LLC
Chambersburg PA
CBHW081519160426
43193CB00015B/2735